MARTIN

MARTIN BENSON SPEAKS

Edited and with an introduction by Carl Lehmann-Haupt

Foreword by Frank R. Sinclair

CODHILL

Codhill Press books
are published for David Appelbaum

First Edition
Printed in the United States of America
Copyright © 2011 by Carl Lehmann-Haupt

ISBN 1-930337-62-0

CONTENTS

Foreword....1

Introduction....7

ONE| *A Vision....33*

TWO| *Talking....35*

THREE| *Childhood....53*

FOUR| *Shocks....77*

FIVE| *War....85*

SIX| *Sound....99*

SEVEN| *Nogent-le-Routrou....109*

EIGHT| *Answering....123*

NINE| *Johnsontown....143*

TEN| *Working....147*

ELEVEN| *The Old Man....169*

TWELVE| *The Ice House....197*

THIRTEEN| *Time....201*

FOURTEEN| *Cloven Hoof Farm....207*

FIFTEEN| *Stories....211*

SIXTEEN| *Thinking....225*

APPENDIX| *A Reading....235*

F O R E W O R D

THE REMARKABLE GREEK-ARMENIAN spiritual master and "teacher of dancing," G. I. Gurdjieff, drew an extraordinary range of people into his orbit—scientists, musicians, physicians, artists, psychologists, philosophers, to name a few. And not the least among these students was an unusual but true son of the soil, Martin Benson. The fascinating trove of reminiscences and reflections contained in this book reflects something of the depth and originality of Benson's understanding of the work for being as conveyed by Gurdjieff. Now, after being kept under wraps for several decades, it is only fitting that Benson's insights can be shared.

Thanks to Carl Lehmann-Haupt, who taped this material during the last months of Benson's life, a pre-publication reading of some excerpts was presented at the 2011 celebration of Gurdjieff's birthday at the Armenian Cathedral in downtown New York. I introduced this material to the listeners, all members and friends of the Gurdjieff Foundation of New York, by sharing some of my own personal recollections of the time I had spent in his company as a young man. What follows is adapted from that slight introduction.

Benson had been the last gatekeeper—and the man who locked the gates for the last time—at the Prieuré, Gurdjieff's estate in Fontainebleau, France, where he had established the Institute for the Harmonious Development of Man. He was later a potent and unorthodox presence at Franklin Farms, the Ouspensky estate in Mendham, New Jersey, during its last few years as a place of Work. And later still he was the presiding spirit in the rather unorthodox ice house at Armonk.

Benson was a man of great simplicity, complexity, and compassion. He had been wounded in action on the Western Front in World War I when hardly out of his teens. Shaken by his experiences, he retreated to the Ramapo Mountains to live among the strange folk of the hills. It was there, as he used to say, that the Work found him, which is a whole untold story in itself.

He was just about to turn 60 when I first encountered him on my arrival at Franklin Farms, in August, 1958. After only a week on the estate, I admitted to Miss Dorothy Darlington, who managed the household that looked after Madame Ouspensky, that I could make neither hide nor hair of what Benson was saying. She assured me that he had indeed spent some time with Gurdjieff, and that Gurdjieff had said of him that he was "more in essence than in personality." This was all very mysterious to me, and I took it as a task to keep an open mind.

For about 18 months I lived under Benson's wing, as it were, working at his side from the crack of dawn often until well after midnight. In the evening, after I had finished my tasks in the main house, he would have me come to his cottage. And there he sat me down and spoke for hours in the same unstructured and unscripted way that comes through in the pages that follow. It was as if he were wrestling in his whole being to find the words to express his search. If I even so much as nodded, as I occasionally did after the long hard day out on the estate, he would poke me in the chest and say, "You don't do that."

And then there came the day when, with the profound compassion and understanding of a man who had himself known suffering, he would acknowledge my own devastating experience of remorse. "You are one of my people," he said. We never ever spoke about that afterwards. But there was clearly a real bond, because one day when I was quietly raking leaves at his cottage he turned to me and said, "Sinclair, I don't know why you came, but I am glad you came."

Although you could not parse his sentences, as Roger Lipsey once said of him in a beautiful poem, Benson was no simpleton, no unlettered bumpkin. But he was certainly not an intellectual either, not remotely a member of the intelligentsia. "Don't make logic," he used to say. And even though his obituary in *The New York Times* said rather imposingly that he was an "agriculturist," he had never regarded himself as anything other than a man who tilled the soil, shoveled manure, wielded an axe with purpose and precision, tended horses and cows and sheep and pigs and chickens—and spoke to them and they to him. He was, in his very marrow, a farmer.

I learned, too, that he loved music, from Bach to songs of the Civil War, and he loved to sing. In fact, on a number of occasions while making my rounds at night, I would find him roaming the grounds during thunderstorms, singing in some strange and nameless tongue to the trees and fields and to the heavens, an elemental man breathing in the vibrant life around him.

After Madame Ouspensky's death at the end of 1961, the Foundation acquired an estate in Armonk. I recall how the brash young Turks of that time, who boasted that they were going to usher in a "new" era in the Work in New York, had no place for Benson in their plans. But he staked his claim to a derelict wooden building known as the ice house, where his loyal stalwarts from the Mendham days installed themselves. The ice house was, as our poet expressed it,

> …a club for heavier men
> Who lumber up the path of consciousness together
> With fair doubts about lighter men elsewhere on the
> grounds….

It was in the ice house that Benson and his crew demonstrated some novel and free-form building techniques, and converted the old brick baking oven into a forge. They straightened and secured the sagging roof by running a rough-hewn tree trunk horizontally down the middle. He used to tell Madame de Salzmann, "That's the Nigerian—we're spearing its jaw." And it was there that this "club for heavier men" continued Benson's passionate exploration of resonance and sound, and built their famous Aeolian or wind harp.

Madame de Salzmann loved the atmosphere of the ice house. After Benson died and his team disbanded, I was allowed to turn the ice house into a print shop, and Madame would come down and just stand to one side watching us at work, not saying anything. Perhaps it was hallowed ground to her as well.

So, now, to hear Benson speak in the rough-hewn way he used to speak. Let the reader brace himself.

—*Frank R. Sinclair, February 1, 2011*

INTRODUCTION
The Man in the Rainbow

MARTIN BENSON SPOKE SO OFTEN about Aeolian harps that one day, near the end of his life, we built him one. When the wind blew over the strings, it picked out the overtones of each note and made them sing, delicately or stridently, according to the wind. On the day he showed the harp to Mme. de Salzmann, there was a slight, occasional breeze circulating in the trees and it drew a few plangent chords from the harp before dying away. We all waited expectantly but nothing stirred. Madame, growing impatient, began to fan the harp with her coattails. It was a charming gesture that spoke to us all. Once you heard that music, you longed to hear it again.

Mr. Benson was innately musical and he perceived the world and its inhabitants in musical terms. He believed that we humans are capable of being attuned to one another, as the strings of an instrument are. When there is sufficient purity of intent in our work together, a significant *sound* may be heard. As he worked with us he was listening for that, and contributing to it as well with the intensity of his effort. "There won't be any sense until you hear that sound," he says on one of the recordings that was made just before he died. Then, sometimes, right in the middle of things, he would stop, and repeat once more the familiar verses from St. John: "The wind bloweth from whence it listeth, and thou hearest the sound thereof." It was his need for a sound like that, one "born of the spirit," that made him say on the tapes, "I want to hear the icehouse ring like an Aeolian harp."

The icehouse was his atelier—Madame called it "the magician's workshop." When the Foundation bought a large property in Armonk, New York in the early Sixties, Benson laid claim to a ramshackle building that had once been an icehouse, shoring it up and piercing the walls with a slender tree trunk to steady the sagging structure. It was there with his small band of followers that he worked at some of the more extreme crafts: blacksmithing, wood bending, glass blowing, and casting bells. At the heart of all that activity was his obsession with sound: sound you can hear—like a bell ringing or a string set vibrating by the wind—and sound you can't so much hear as intuit or sense.

When visitors from abroad would come looking for him down at the icehouse he would sometimes conduct a demonstration. One of his people would bring out a small brass bell they'd cast and Mr. Benson would tap it smartly on the rim. Then everyone would listen as the clear ping died out. When the sound was gone, the visitor would be invited to take the edge of the bell between thumb and forefinger. It never failed to astonish. The bell was still vibrating; you could *touch* the sound you could no longer hear. Then Benson might be moved to say the lines Keats wrote about the sweetness of unheard music.

Martin Benson died in December, 1971. At the reception after the funeral, Jack Moscrop was very excited. Jack was one of Mr. Benson's icehouse people and he thought he'd seen something important when he looked into the coffin. "He caught the moment of death," he declared. He was all keyed up and he said it again: "I saw it in his face; he *caught* the moment of death." I wondered about that afterwards. Was it possible to witness one's own death? Wouldn't you have to be alive to do that? Did he mean that Mr. Benson was somehow still alive as he died? I thought of the vibrating bell. Did it mean that if we *listened* in the way Martin Benson taught we would be able to feel his force and vitality vibrating still, even after the sound of his voice had died out?

It was that force and vitality one noticed first. He was magnetic. Lincoln Kirstein, writing in his autobiography, describes meeting him when he visited the Prieuré in the summer of 1927: "a blond American, as solid as a draft horse." When Benson invited Kirstein to work with him that day, Kirstein felt something light up. "A surge of well being rushed up from somewhere to overwhelm me." A bit later he adds, "This blessing of limitless capacity I felt at Le Prieuré was not entirely identified with Martin Benson, although he magnetized and focused it." That was an important distinction: the force that emanated from Mr. Benson came both from and through him, a combination of his own natural exuberance and the force of the Teaching. "The reason you're in this kind of work," he once said, in answer to someone's question, "is that this has more force than you do. Therefore you will be part of it in order to help you gain more force. Once you have accepted this work, you have taken a part of a force that actually does not belong to you. You have taken a part of God's force. Because this is His job, if you want to know—to pull people together. You have taken a part of this force upon yourself. And forever and ever and ever you are both blessed and cursed."

Just as Lincoln Kirstein had forty years earlier, I too, came under Mr. Benson's spell. The year was 1965, and I remember walking with him and his wife across the lawn behind the house that they'd just bought in Mt. Kisco. That is, the house that *she*, his wife, Mrs. Benson, had bought. He scarcely noticed that there *was* a house on that property. What he had bought was a little valley so protected from the surrounding neighborhood it almost seemed to be in wilderness, rather than the hundred yards from the Saw Mill River Parkway and forty-five minutes from downtown Manhattan that it actually was. What he had bought was the solitude and the quiet and the trees and the animals that would become his intimate friends in the last years of his life. As we walked, Mr. Benson made a little leap as if to click his heels. "I'm a spring chicken," he said. It was a delightful exuberance. Only much later would I appreciate all that he had packed into that leap and ejaculation.

INTRODUCTION

I was just a kid back then, a graduate student with a part time teaching job. He was 67, a retired farmer with a precise idea of how he wanted to live in the last stage of his remarkable life. He wanted time to think. He wanted the solitude the little valley afforded as a condition for that thinking. And there were other things he wanted to do, too — various experiments he wanted to conduct with sound and listening. I decided to spend all the time I could in the company of this singular man, so I made myself his gardener. Every Saturday I traveled to Mt. Kisco where I mowed the lawn or cut the firewood. In the spring I dug and planted the garden; in the fall I raked the leaves. There were others, of course, who worked at other things. Mr. Benson would stand, watching and directing, and tell us his stories.

Telling stories was his way of working with us. The stories made connections that affected us, affected the way we thought and felt about what we were doing, and changed the way our muscles moved our bones. One spring, after runoff from melting snow had flooded his basement, he asked a couple of us to dig a trench to drain the water away from the house. Our trench was only about a foot deep, but as we dug he told us about the Culebra Cut, the artificial valley that American engineers had dug between 1904 and 1914 to connect the Atlantic and Pacific oceans across the continental divide in Panama. He told us about the immensity of the enterprise; how, even before the Americans took over from the French, more than 22,000 people had died, sick with malaria or yellow fever, or drowned in the endlessly shifting mudslides.

Our little trench gained something from that association; our shovels felt different in our hands. We could feel a relation of scale—how something small could be related to something almost unimaginably huge. The relation to a greater scale of things—an incommensurably greater scale of time and spaciousness—was essential to his understanding of the way the Work could shock people into wakefulness.

Martin Benson was a different kind of teacher and his approach to the Work differed from the more psychological one practiced by some of Gurdjieff's other pupils. The strength of mind required to hold his own against the sophisticated, Oxford-educated British who had accompanied Ouspensky to the States during the Second World War can only be imagined. "This is not the Gurdjieff Work anymore," he complained to Mme. de Salzmann. "We should change the name from the Gurdjieff Foundation to the British Ouspensky People in America Foundation." He didn't believe in psychological exercises. He didn't think you could come to a state of attention by closing your eyes in a quiet place at an appointed time. "You all talk about attention," he said, "but you haven't got the power to come to a real attention, just by yourself." He believed that one had to be put on the spot and shocked before one would be able to attend productively. "We're not capable. We're not weak, but we're not capable until there's a hell of a big shock—a big shock that'll come and hit us and throw us right off balance, and within that could be the answer."

Once I found him standing alone outside the cabin in the upper field. I came up behind him as he was looking at a log he'd dragged out of the forest. "Oh, hello Carl," he said, unsurprised to see me appear out of nowhere. "Give me a hand with this log, won't you?" The log was ten or twelve feet long, partially rotted, its bark host to a green moss and a variety of boring insects. Together we heaved it onto a pair of sawhorses and stripped it, sawed off the stubs of branches, and gouged out its rotten patches until all the wood showed fresh and green and smooth. Then he had me knot a rope to one end of the log and throw the free end over a high branch on a tree. We hoisted the log till it swung free, at which point he thwacked it with a stick. *Thump.* The log made a dull muffled thud that disappointed me. It was nothing like the ringing crack I thought he was expecting. I felt disappointed for him, but he didn't seem the least concerned. Only years later did I perceive what he'd intended me to understand. We had enacted a metaphor for "work on oneself"—cleaning, stripping, hollowing oneself out until one became sufficiently resonant to contain the unheard reverberation that the World makes within us.

"It's not like listening for a bell," he told Mme. de Salzmann. "But to hear that sound—there's a definite sound there—and until you do, you don't know if you're coming or going. It's all mixed up. There won't be any sense until you hear that sound. If you can hear that sound, no matter what happens, it'll be right."

Whether answering questions at a Sunday lunch or speaking informally to us as we worked around his place, there were always the stories—stories he told again and again, though never in the same way twice. There were stories from his life, from his time at the Prieuré with Mr. Gurdjieff, and from his childhood growing up around the old port of New York; and then there were stories from his wide reading in history and geology. There was nothing scholarly about his reading; he'd had scant formal education. But the past was an essential part of his nature. Even as a child he was gifted with historical vision. He often told us how, when he was only ten or eleven, he'd been lying at the edge of a cliff up in the Catskill Mountains looking out over a wide vista, when he saw, as in a dream, one civilization after another, each with its distinctive architectural style, rise up and pass before his eyes.

The past echoed in him; the tissue of history, wars, migrations, the collapse of empires, all seemed woven into his being. He couldn't understand why he felt so keenly about the Civil War, as if he'd been present at the Bloody Angle where the bullets flew like hail and sawed the trees in two, or had followed Lee's army "walking backwards" on the long retreat to Appomattox. And the songs of the Hebrides Islands pierced his heart as if he'd been born there at another time. Later, when he read Octavio Paz's great book on Levi-Strauss, it was the "cyclical time" of so-called primitive tribes that came to occupy his thoughts deeply. He felt the Work could not be understood within our Western sense of time. He asked us to probe the question, "What in your mind is time?" Benson must have pondered this passage from the Paz book many times:

"None the less, something separates us from that world; affectivity. The savage feels himself to be a part of nature and asserts his fraternity with the animal species; we [Westerners] affirm the singularity and exclusivity of the human species for being the only one that has a history and knows it. More sober and more wise, primitives distrust history because they see in it the beginning of the separation, the beginning of the exile of man adrift in the cosmos."

Sometimes, while I hoed in the garden, he would perch on a chair and tell me about his delving into geology. He seemed to sense the crust of the earth as if it were alive, his bones attuned to the slippage of continental plates and to the long rhythmic pulse of moving glaciers. He had a word store in his mind as well, a compendium of sentences he'd gathered from his eclectic reading: the Old Testament, the Elizabethans, Addison, Lincoln, Melville, Joyce and poets like Whitman and Sydney Lanier (whose family he had known). "All the flowers of the spring," he would say, smiling, quoting Webster's Duchess of Malfi, "come to bedeck my burying."

As we listened to him talk, the present seemed to dissolve. He remembered an earlier island than the Manhattan we know today, the same one Melville knew, "belted round by wharves as Indian isles by coral reefs," and he would describe what it was like to walk along South Street when the bowsprits of the tall ships reached almost to the house fronts on the opposite side. He remembered how, when he'd shipped out in 1917, his company had been issued capes left over from the Civil War. And how, when his platoon, stationed in an old Napoleonic barracks in Belgium, got lousy, it was with the descendents of lice from wars a century before. He told us how he studied horse breeding after the War on a farm in La Beauce where they bred the great Percheron draft horses whose forebears had borne the fully-armored knights of the Frankish armies against Islamic invaders at the Battle of Poitiers in 732. When Mr. Benson pointed to the boulder beneath which he wished his ashes to be strewn, he knew it had been placed by the last glacier that had scraped out the little valley ten thousand years earlier.

Listening to him was like riding a small raft over the rapids. His sentences veered and plunged, but you hung on. You knew you were getting the shocks of an authentic teaching, conveyed in an entirely idiosyncratic way and it didn't matter if, like me, you were too young and inexperienced to assimilate it on the spot. You might not get the point, but you could hear the greatness and wonder in his voice. The Work he spoke of was no hand-me-down; he had made it his own and he always encouraged his listeners to do the same. You've got to "make your own expression," he insisted, even as he did himself.

Talking in the way he did seemed natural, but by his own account it came hard and late; he only learned to speak freely about the Work late in his life. "For many, many years I was absolutely frozen," he told us. "I could not talk at all to anybody about the Work." Whenever he tried to organize his ideas in advance or write out his thoughts, he was so utterly unschooled that he couldn't do it. And because he was essentially a storyteller, his talk was subject to the temptations of improvised narration—lurching mid-sentence digressions, solecisms, clumsy repetitions and wild leaps. Whatever he thought of he simply added to the mix. Giving his tongue free rein to ramble and veer allowed him to align himself with the shocking scale and power of his understanding. "Knowing isn't my best force," he said. "Not knowing, just *not* knowing (but knowing) is. Whatever I can draw upon, that is where I am. That is my position. The depth of my knowledge is there. It's stored in a place in my being from where, if I'm honest with the situation, I'll just talk and let it come out. I don't care anymore what comes out. It's not intellectually thought out, or correct." When he at last found a way to speak, it was because he'd ceased to be concerned with the logical expression of what he was saying. When he turned his attention entirely to the sensation and feel of what he was talking about, his subject could shock him into articulate speech. "[My way] is different," he would say, "and probably crazier than most people's, because I'm working on the subject as I'm talking, through myself, and not through one possible center. I'm trying to say these things through my whole self. And that's why some very good things can happen, and some God-awful things can happen."

About a year before Mr. Benson died, I asked him if he'd allow me to record some of his stories. I'd drive out from the city on a weekday evening when I knew he'd be alone and fix a light dinner (he seemed to live on Snow's Clam Chowder). Afterwards we'd move to the living room where we'd crack the first of several beers and begin. He soon grew so comfortable with the little tape recorder that I began turning it on in other circumstances, though always only at his place—in group meetings at the cabin and at group dinners on his front porch. When we were alone he mostly reminisced; in group meetings he tried to address a person's question directly; and at dinners he was inclined to hold forth about whatever was on his mind at the moment.

He said of our recording sessions together: "They're a wonderful exercise for me." But he never expressed any interest in the form a book about his life might take. Nonetheless he wished to convey something beyond the facts of his existence. He had an elevated concept of what is possible for each of us. If someone, somewhere, had succeeded in expressing something, then that expression was within anyone's reach. "If another man has done it," he once said, "I can do it." As he told us stories from his life, he told them with wonder—wonder that he was alive, that he was "living tissue," as he liked to say. "If you are to write something of your life's story, you have to remember something of the greater thing that could be than just that, because that's not the shock that I'd like to put forward. The shock would be something that I'm striving toward and for, in a general way, not in my wacky way, because there's no direction in my way, and I don't want any direction. I don't think any good thoughts come in a directed line."

In my effort to organize the sprawling transcripts that Stanley Isaacs and Marshall May prepared from the tapes, I have kept his aim in mind: the striving to convey, even at this far remove in time and place, the shock that his inimitable "expression" of the Work can still deliver. I have, for that reason, divided his narrative into two distinct streams: one, autobiographical; the other, edifying. In the first, the reader will find chapters about separate periods of Mr. Benson's life—his childhood, the war, horse breeding in France, his time at the Prieuré, etc. Alternating with these are chapters called, variously, *Talking, Shocks, Working,* etc., in which he exhorts and explains.

Although he was, at the end of his life, the stubborn, fierce protector of his idiosyncratic style, Mr. Benson did not hold himself in high regard. He often lamented that he'd fallen short: "Something more should have come of it," he'd say, or, "I'm such a failure." We tried, without really understanding what he meant, to honor and assure him. But praise of the sort we could muster, coming from the choir, was cold comfort to a man of such visionary ambitions. On the other hand, he never lost his deft turn of mind and lightness of spirit, as the following exchange with his wife will show.

Mrs. Benson: My husband spends all his time regretting that he is not Leonardo da Vinci or someone equally remarkable. He goes through such regrets.

Mr. Benson: I not only go through such regrets, I feel like such a sap. I really do. And I am a sap.

Mrs. Benson: He doesn't feel enough has been accomplished.

Mr. Benson: It's not accomplishments; it's my growth that is not accomplished. That is the thing that I think of more. I should have grown... with all the things that I have delved into I should have....

Mrs. Benson: The key to something.

Mr. Benson: A lot... I haven't got a lot. Anyhow, let's get drunk. Sköl! I mean, more or less we can change the subject. I hate to see young girls suffer—I'm pure of heart.

Although none of the notes and fragmentary comments we found around the house after he died, inscribed on scraps of lined notebook paper and backs of envelopes, embodied great writing, they all testified to his love of exalted language. (All of these have since been lost.) It isn't difficult to imagine that he would have liked to write something grand. I once heard someone say that Mr. Benson wanted to write "scripture," as part of a three-point program he'd purportedly set himself. In the first stage, he would learn to bend wood with live steam. (Two elegant sleds were made, with curving runners made of oak.) In the second, he planned to make an Aeolian harp. It pleased him mightily that the one Ken Ward and I built for him came from plans that a seventeenth-century Jesuit priest and polymath, Athanasius Kircher, had drawn. In the third stage, he wanted to write "scripture." If the fact that he never succeeded at such a task caused his disappointment, one may well ask: who then is not a failure?

Speaking into the tape recorder filled a need. It was *something*—a straw to grasp, a place to house some part of the "residue" he wished to leave. He certainly had no illusions. He knew that his way of speaking couldn't be transcribed.

Still, he would have his say. What you will read here is only a pale approximation of his speaking voice, but for those who knew him, and for others too perhaps, it will give some intimation of his incomparable way of working and teaching.

■ ■ ■

Martin Benson's life began with a shock. In the months just prior to his birth and just before the turning of the old century, the family learned that his father and uncle had been drowned off the Cape of Good Hope. Both men were ship's captains who owned the vessels they commanded; when their ships foundered in a storm, the entire family was financially ruined. Up until then, his substantial, Swedish, sea-faring family lived comfortably on Henry Street in Brooklyn Heights. His mother's mother had been the first woman doctor in Sweden. Her daughter, who'd come to New York as a young bride, bore four children. Besides Benson, the youngest, there was a brother, older by nine years, a sister who died at an early age, and a second sister who raised Benson when his mother was forced to go to work as a nurse to support the family.

The family must have moved to Carroll Gardens early on, for it was in Carroll Park that he found "his tree," the large oak under which his sister learned to look for him each time he mysteriously disappeared when he was still only three or four. He grew up "pretty wild," as he would say—fatherless and poor. While his brother went on to become "a famous engineer," Benson stopped school when he was fourteen or fifteen. Afterwards he apparently lived for a time alone in the Catskills, in a cabin he had built for himself. When the country entered the War in 1917, he lied about his age and enlisted in the Pioneer Infantry. As a teenager, he seems also to have spent some time with his mother in Maine, where he learned to raise pigs. "Pigs are wonderful," he liked to say. "People should know about pigs. They're the most intelligent of all the animals."

When he decided to become a farmer and never go to sea, it outraged the family and the "captains" who came to drink and feast on Christmas Eve. For them, there could be nothing lower than a farmer. But having his feet rooted firmly in the earth must have had some special meaning for the child who'd lost his father to the sea. Even very late in life he told us, rather proudly, that on his last visit to France he had told the haughty Pauline de Dampierre that she needed to keep her feet on the ground.

While farming was the career he chose, he had early intimations of his calling to "something greater." There was that tree in Carrol Park for one thing—his first intuition of the healing power of natural forces—and the vision in the Catskills, for another, that taught him to regard historical time in a larger perspective. And of course there was his essentially musical experience of the world. Although he would train himself to become a farmer, not a historian or musician, the great movements of history were in continuous operation in his mind and the investigation of sound would become the singular focus of his life at the end.

He told us of a terrible shock he got while fighting on the Belgian front. Seeing an Allied soldier fall between the lines, he left the relative safety of the trenches to gather the wounded man onto his shoulders and carry him back, but a German rifleman shot the man dead as he was rescuing him. The incident left him with a double burden of remorse. Not only had the man's dead body shielded him under fire, but he would always wonder if the man might not have lived if he hadn't tried to rescue him. His sorrow was overwhelming. When he arrived at the Prieuré, he asked Mr. Gurdjieff if the memory of the event would ever leave him and Gurdjieff told him he would carry it forever. Many years later he still wept when he recalled it.

After the war, he seems to have enrolled briefly at the University of New Hampshire's agricultural school, before quitting in disgust over the poor instruction. He then found his way back to France and for two years, as a ward of the French Government, studied horse breeding on a large farm in Nogent-le-Retrou, where he was known as "White Mountain" because of his blond hair and great size. A few years after Mr. Benson died, I paid a visit to Robert Avaline, the son of "le patron," with whom he'd raised so much hell that they were both thrown in jail on more than one occasion. Now a prosperous (and rather self-satisfied) banker, he seemed immured in his success, and the vivid adventures that burned brightly in Benson's memory had mostly faded in his.

One winter shortly after the war, he built himself a cabin near Johnsontown, New York, in an area that is now part of Harriman State Park. He'd been gassed at Passchendaele Ridge and needed to clear his lungs. A friend I met at Mr.

Benson's funeral had spent time with him there and told me that they shot and ate so many squirrels that winter that, as he put it, "We *smelled* like squirrels." He made good contact with the hill people, the "Jackson Whites," who were famously disinclined to trust outsiders. "Them's violets, Ben," one of these tough, distrustful men said to him one day as he handed Benson an early spring bouquet.

The Work "found him," as he put it, after the Herald Tribune had run a story about his life in the hills. Someone in the Orage group read it and, sensing a candidate for the Teaching, took it upon himself to trek all the way in to Benson's cabin on snowshoes in the dead of winter to tell him about the Work. (Benson never said much about Orage, though his thinking was clearly influenced by him.) The next time we see Benson he's become gatekeeper at the Prieuré, and Gurdjieff, still in bandages from his 1924 automobile accident, is limping up the path toward him.

Mr. Benson's stories about Gurdjieff, which we heard many times and in many variations, offer a singular perspective on his teacher's way of working. I have reproduced them here as they appear on the tapes, but I recall stories that were never recorded. When I was asked to prepare a reading from the Benson material for the January 13th celebration at St. Vartan's Cathedral in 2011, I made a highly edited version into which I interpolated sentences I knew by heart but that were not on the tapes. That reading offers a more focused version of Mr. Benson's stories about Gurdjieff and I have reproduced the text of it in an Appendix.

To give just one example of this kind of interpolation: the photograph on the cover of this book shows Mr. Benson and his wife, Rita Romilly, on their wedding day. A smiling Gurdjieff is posed between them, one arm around the shoulder of each. The wedding took place in Stamford, Connecticut, in a church where Orage had been married; Mr. Gurdjieff came up especially for the occasion. When the minister asked him about his relation to the bride and groom he replied, "I father both." Although we'd heard the story many times, it was never recorded. It was, however, imprinted on our minds, and if I include it—illegally, as it were—it is because it is too good to lose. Mr. Gurdjieff's three words speak volumes about how close he was to his two pupils.

The Bensons' was an unlikely marriage. (I heard one unsympathetic colleague comment that Mrs. Benson "had caught the last man out of the Prieuré.") While Benson was a vital and attractive man, there was nothing sophisticated about him. He was, after all, a farmer. Left to his own devices, he'd choose to wear a blue work shirt buttoned up to the collar. His wife, however, preferred to call him an *agriculturist* and bought him clothes at Brooks Brothers. That was because she *was* sophisticated. When she was younger she'd been a skilled socialite as well as a trained actress who liked to claim—inaccurately, as the record later showed—that she had been George M. Cohan's leading lady. She had been actively in touch with the artists, performers and writers of the time, and opened her house on Sutton Place to them on many an evening. Jacob Epstein recorded that he heard Paul Robeson sing there. Carl Van Vechten had photographed the young couple against elaborate floral wall-paper that covered her walls. (She was also a skilled decorator). She taught acting for many years at the American Academy and when Robeson was chosen to play Othello in a Broadway production in 1943, she was his drama coach. (Robeson received a Gold Medal for the best diction in the American theater for that role.) When I knew her, there were drawings and etchings by Picasso and Matisse on the wall above her sofa, as well as a large Calder drawing that was dedicated in his hand to "Rita and Martin." On a pedestal by a window was a cast bronze of a baby's head that Epstein had made.

Though she never said as much, I think the presence of the child's head in her collection had special significance. In 1938 she was pregnant with a son, but the child was stillborn. She was mad with grief, and when a well-meaning nurse brought the dead infant for her to see, she tried to throw herself out the window. Strangely Mr. Benson never mentioned the loss of the child. Then, only a few years later, another sorrow would follow.

Soon after they married, the Bensons bought a farm in Washington, Connecticut, that he named "Cloven Hoof Farm," presumably because he planned to raise goats on it, but in 1943 or '44 the house burned to the ground. In the space of just a few years, all their plans for the future had been blighted. With some bitterness Mr. Benson said he never wanted to own anything again as long as he lived.

The years during the Second World War were hard. "It was like a visitation," he said. "One damn thing after another happened. I became very ill during the War. I had lobar pneumonia, and then I had two serious operations within five days, which almost killed me. I think these things upset me." While working in the Bethlehem shipyards, he'd gotten sick on a hospital ship he was testing (" ... submarines all over the god-damned place ... ") and took eight months to fully recover.

In 1946 he went west by himself, to Oregon and Washington, with the idea of starting a group and maybe home-steading. He lived in Eugene for a time and sat up late on the front steps of the fraternity houses at the University talking with young men recently returned from the War. Later Mrs. Benson joined him and together they explored the possibility of buying an island in Puget Sound and farming it. They returned to New York in 1949 when they received news of Mr. Gurdjieff's death.

Rumors of Mr. Benson had reached me long before we met. I was working with a French group outside Paris at the time Mme. Ouspensky died in December of 1961, and the next summer a contingent of the French were invited to the last Work period at Franklin Farms. When I asked the architect/builder Michel Kalt what had impressed him most in the New World, he shot back, "Martin Benson! Cet homme imperturbable dans son petit chapeau mou." And he went on to say how easily he could imagine Benson's sitting at the foot of the Grande Coulee dam while just over his head they poured a thousand tons of cement. "He wouldn't bat an eyelash," Kalt said admiringly.

After Gurdjieff's death Mme. de Salzmann undertook the daunting task of reconciling the differing Work groups in and around New York—the Ouspenskyites based at Franklin Farms in Mendham, New Jersey, and the Gurdjieff/Orage groups in the City. Bill Segal described Madame's skill in reconciling the groups as "sheer wizardry." One of her strategies was to send Martin Benson to live at Franklin Farms because, although he was vehemently "anti-Ouspensky," he was a person who, as Segal (an Ouspenskyite) puts it, "we could all like." The Bensons took over the Gate Cottage; he began to raise pigs and chickens. It was here that he persuaded a chicken to adopt a litter of orphan pigs.

There is another story from Mendham that captures the essence of the man I knew. Martha Heyneman describes how once when she was working in the kitchen with some others during a fierce thunderstorm, Mr. Benson came in to warn them not to touch the water faucets. To this eminently practical advice he added his report of how he himself had been walking in the rain and seen a rainbow that came down in a nearby field of Jerusalem artichokes. Based on the story, Martha wrote the poem "Martin Benson at Franklin Farms." Here are its concluding lines.

> *"And what he has to tell us—*
> *in addition to the warning that the lightning will*
> *   come streaking*
> *down the water-pipes and knock us girls all dead—*
> *   is how ·*
> *he has been outside walking inside a rainbow.*

"The end of it
came past down by the artichokes," he says,
"so I ran and got inside and stayed inside—
crashed through the hedge and crossed the road
inside and heard brakes
and somebody shouting, "My God!"

"There goes a man inside a rainbow!"

■ ■ ■

Martin Benson died standing up. We carried his coffin into the church "feet first," the same way he went into any new undertaking. After the funeral, Ken Ward and I followed the coffin to the crematorium. Driving west across the park, something uncanny occurred: a young man mounted bareback on a huge, white draft horse entered the line of traffic directly in front of the hearse while seemingly out of nowhere a man in kilts with a bagpipe appeared. We proceeded, solemnly and majestically, now led by the horse and rider, as far as the Park's exit, while the piper stood playing "Who wouldna fecht wi' Charlie." It was as if the world had paused for a moment to salute Benson's passing.

For many years the tapes we made lay in a cardboard box at the back of a closet. Then Stanley Isaacs volunteered to transcribe them and still later Marshall May made a digital version. I edited the text in the form you will read. The same thought occurred to each of us as we worked: we understood our teacher in ways we never did when he was among us. We understood the lonely and courageous battle he'd fought for his vision of the Work. Surrounded as he was by men and women who had more education and spoke more fluently and had more money, he adhered to his essential understanding that the Work would only survive by being made new. Again and again he would ask; "What is your expression?" and with his question he intended that each person undertake to express the Work in a way that was essentially his own and not the imitation of the Teacher that so many attempted.

The key to his work was his investigation of sound, and of a way of listening and attending to it that was original to him. He was naturally musical, so innocently gifted that it came as a shock to him that not everyone had perfect pitch. Even as a child he was known for his singing — neighborhood children tormented him by calling him "Martin Caruso" — and he knew the hymns backwards and forwards, and through them was introduced to Bach, Handel and Haydn. As a young man he'd haunted Carnegie Hall and boasted that he could replay anything on the piano at home that he'd heard at a concert. But that was the extent of his musical training. Whatever he knew about music was instinctive. A big oak organ stood to one side of the dining room at his house in Mt. Kisco but I never heard him play it or sing. On the tapes he says a very strange thing: he says he'd "graduated" from music.

It's hard to reconcile this assertion with his love of music. There were times I surprised him as he was listening to a recording of the Tuskegee Choir, and the face he turned to me as I entered the room was one transformed by deep emotion.

Read his description of the brass ensemble he heard playing Bach from the choir loft at Notre Dame. Is it possible to
"graduate" from a love of the sublime in music to the sound
of a Tibetan bell or the dull thump of a stick hitting a log?
But that is his claim, and it led him to the practice of another,
greater, order of listening. "...that's why I'm fooling around
with tone," he says on one tape. "I think you have to hear
tones as no one else hears them."

Strike a note and listen. With practice you can learn to distinguish the range of overtones within that single note. Recall
then the concept of the creation as a continuum of pulsing
matter, extending upward by degrees from the "firm calm"
of a nearly insensate materiality to an "absolute" of nearly
immaterial intensity. At every level there is manifest some
degree of "mind," some measure of sentience, intelligence,
or conscious awareness; a great chain of being that leads
through humans to whatever lies beyond the "phenomenon
of man"—planets, suns, galaxies and so forth. Everything in
the material universe carries a spiritual "charge," a certain
quality of energy animating it. Humans bear a special responsibility in this scheme, a duty to distinguish the concealed life
in each thing and make it more distinct. We must persistently
strive to "listen" more acutely, a listening that I conceive to be
the effort to conform our attention to the higher and higher
frequencies that are both immanent in us and at large in the
world. At the end, Benson spoke a lot about what he called
"the void." I think he meant that the work of attention is
not only toward *presence* but also in the direction of what

lies beyond presence and beyond being. There is no *end* to our striving. Yet it is a striving that is recognized, finally, as a commandment for those humans whose home address is the planet earth.

When I listen again, in memory, to Martin Benson's voice saying "I'm a spring chicken," I hear the fundamental note from which his saying sprang. He knew how to channel what he called "the natural forces." He had graduated to a level of endeavor that I couldn't imagine at the time, and his little leap was the outward and visible sign of his development. It said, "I have the force of things that originate within themselves and nothing, not death itself, can stop me in my flight."

1 | A VISION

*"A person approaching consciousness
would probably be considered crazy."*

"THIS IS WHAT I MEAN. I think you're born that way. I was pretty crazy when I was a child. I used to go off by myself when I was three years old. I had a park, and that was *my* park. I had a tree, and every time I was gone they would know where I was—they'd find me under the tree. I would seek these things out. When I was eleven, up in the Catskill Mountains, I was on a large cliff overlooking hundreds of miles of big mountains, and I was just resting like this, when I really had a vision. I had never been with books enough to see what civilizations looked like, or had been, or anything. It never made any connection with me—I had never seen them. But while I was there, I saw whole civilizations, like a panorama that swept over me, but on a big cliff, overlooking miles...I was lying down...one civilization after another passed before me—one after another, different kinds of architecture. This went on and on. For years I remembered every one of these damn things. Now, if I wasn't open to that kind of thing, this would never have happened. I could never, never imagine such a thing, because I didn't have access to this kind of thing. That impressed me so. I didn't know what was happening to me, but that was a deep-rooted vision. And I wasn't asleep. I was wide-awake. And that was my vision. I experienced a vision. When I tell people to seek their vision—and seeing something like that could happen—they don't know what you're talking about because they have not experienced it."

"I know where I had my various visions growing up. I know every damn step of that. But to have things happening at all times is absolutely impossible, I think. I could never create the vision. Your whole metabolism, your whole inside has to be in a kind of conjunction that would make it possible. Suddenly this thing would be illuminated. I think, in a curious way, that's where that word comes from. It's more than an event—you see something."

"I could never, never imagine such a thing, because I didn't have access to this kind of thing. That impressed me so. I didn't know what was happening to me, but that was a deep-rooted vision. And I wasn't asleep, I was wide-awake. As a matter of fact, I threw myself down; I was leaning, overlooking a big space up in the Catskill Mountains."

2 | *TALKING*

"I could not talk at all, to anybody, about the Work."

"NOW, THAT'S WHY we have these gatherings, these meetings. We attack the problem in different ways; mine is different and probably crazier than most people's, because I'm working on the subject as I'm talking, through myself, and not through one possible center. I'm trying to say these things through my whole self, and that's why some very good things can happen. God knows, I don't say that egotistically, but some very good things can happen, and some God-awful things can happen. That's when certain things don't click and mesh like a watch; the wheels and things don't go."

"There have been moments when certain forms of the arts expressed a way of life, not just an art expression. It was a way of existence, where many people put their whole heart, soul, and life into this kind of performance. One example was Mt. Saint Michel. It was a monastic fortification, a cathedral, on a rock in the English Channel. The tide comes in about forty feet and goes out leaving ten or fifteen miles of sand. The only way to get to the rock was over a causeway, and there's not a stone in that whole country. The people from the surrounding country went religiously to pick up stones in the French Jura Mountains. They hauled thirteen-foot cubes by oxen, dragged them over and through swamps and rivers, and killed off everything for this cathedral. That was done as religiously, as objectively, as I could possibly imagine, by groups of people. Each stone has a little mark telling what guild or what little township went off to get a stone—one stone for their cathedral. It took a thousand years for the building; most of the people who had something to do with it never saw it finished. That is not happening today. We have lost that kind of thing, because we have another medium of exchange, and it's crippling us a great deal instead of helping us develop objectively and towards something. Now we have this exchange of money—an exchange of money instead of human development."

"Someone in the other group asked me about freedom. It's a very difficult question until you understand the situation. These people were free. They were free deeply inside in order to do something greater than they were. You're never free of anything, only free to do something else. I didn't mean to talk about that, but this came into it. You should learn some of the difference between what is valuable and what is not valuable. Do not waste your time on this, that, and the other thing—if you do something as objectively as possible, with your whole being, then everything, as they always say about Christianity (I hate to use the term), shall be added unto you."

"The Work, our Work, is so vast that there are many facets to it. It's on a vast, vast scale. This is an idea that I knew for years and years—and I always say this because I recognize it—my sense of time, that I had never solved in any way. I couldn't solve it; I didn't know enough. I'm beginning to solve it, and gain a feeling for a greater scope of time than just the ordinary time that I live in. That hasn't much to do with you, but you will find that out if you do a great research within yourself. The time that you live in today is not the time that we're talking about. It doesn't fit ordinary time. Ordinary conversation doesn't fit the Work. The ordinary sense doesn't fit."

"It has to be done on an extraordinary basis, like that, and almost immediately it will show you where you are in your knowledge and your understanding. You draw upon these things in order to express something that you know about but the depth of that conversation is where you are. I may be that far, I may be this far, and this kind of thing is my possibility of scale of development."

"Don't pass anything along until …. Why pass anything along until you are more or less ready to pass something on? As I said before, no one has to know anything. What you're going through…we're all going through something great. One of the reasons I'm talking to you tonight is to show some places where you won't lose twenty years, where you won't lose a hell of a lot of time because you're frozen, you're stuck, you don't know what to do."

"Now, in this knowing of something to do, you live in a kind of hell until you arrive at this thing, either by yourself or by chance and accident. For many, many years I was absolutely frozen. I could not talk at all, to anybody, about the Work. I didn't know what the hell I was talking about in the first place, and I was frozen in front of the group, an audience. And so nothing, nothing could come. Then I thought of planning a talk and that was more disastrous. To learn this kind of process took a long, long time, until I came to the final conclusion that I was unable to prepare. Then I had to get to the point of saying to myself, hot or cold, I throw myself into this frozen ocean and start talking, and whatever comes out, comes out."

"That is something to try. I could not see two words connected—one word, followed by another word. It just did not happen that easily for me, and I suffered like hell. But that doesn't matter. I found out that if I talk at Armonk, or in France, in front of two hundred Frenchmen who don't understand American English, I cannot feel licked. That is when you get your big shock! And that is when you're on the spot. You're put on the spot because you're unable to do it yourself. You have to recognize this process. You can't walk out. As soon as I was put on the spot in France—that was one of the wildest things I ever went through—in a foreign country with a lot of foreigners, Frenchmen, listening to me, and Mme. de Salzmann sitting beside me. I talked, like that. You're on the spot, no matter what is produced."

"This is why I could help alleviate some of your pressures, by relating what happened to me. Maybe not, maybe you have your own experience. What is produced, that is where I am; that is where I am in my truth and my knowledge of things and my understanding of things, without fear, absolutely fearless. That's the thing to learn. Here I was, so full of fears about what everybody else was going to think or say or do or what. I was absolutely lost, but it wasn't only that—I just couldn't do it because I didn't have this understanding that I am unable to prepare, because I could never remember what I prepared."

"Now I call on another force, a force that is my own, within me, in order to produce. And it'll all be done in simple form. That is one of the reasons that I can help you overcome that kind of thing. Not that you should talk—why do you want to tell anybody unless you have a good reason? But one thing I will say to you, regarding aim: unless you do something everyday as objectively as possible toward that aim, and you really believe in your aim, deep down, nothing will come of it, or very little. If you do something toward it, it will grow, and you'll begin to fulfill your aim. Nobody has to know what your aim is."

"I probably shouldn't say this, but there's a part in the Ouspensky book [*In Search of the Miraculous*] that says that the teacher or the master or whatever he calls himself—Ouspensky—should know the person's aim. This is absolutely untrue. If Mr. Ouspensky was alive, I'd tell him. I've had it out with Mme. de Salzmann many times. I said, 'This is not us.' There are two schools of thought there; one was the Ouspensky group, and one was the Gurdjieff group. We were not supposed to reveal our aim because that's us. That's your own conviction, and you should attempt to fulfill it."

"You see, you shouldn't make 'ordinary sense' of things. If you are going to express something deeply of this Work, you'll do it in another sense, and your other sense will tell you to think three or four times before you make that expression to people who are using their ordinary senses. That's why I say, 'Be careful of what the hell you say.'"

"I don't know if you like these talks. They're a wonderful exercise for me. But I can give you all the information in the world, and it won't mean anything until you start something for yourself. It comes to you, that which we call our own polarity, and then you have the possibility of recalling almost anything you wish to recall. That's what I have the possibility of doing. I'm getting away from this kind of civilized time. That's the way I was raised, on this time, and that was my disaster. I didn't know what the hell was wrong until I actually caught up with it by staying with it. When I actually saw it written and I figured it out, and when I saw it within myself, I said, 'That's it. That's my misunderstanding with myself.' You'll come upon these things, and no one can answer you—stay with it, and if you find it, that is something. You feel just like a bastard all the time, the way you're floundering around, but it can be found."

"The thing I work on is another theory that may be absolutely wrong, and that is about the impressions I take in and retain. It isn't a question of remembering. When I'm talking, say on a Sunday at Armonk, and I need certain material, I can recall that memory. I didn't remember it, there it is. And sometimes it's screwy. I don't care anymore; I really don't care. That gives me leeway. This happens to me, though not all the time. I have it. It's within me. It's not on the tip of my tongue."

"On Sundays at Armonk, I don't know a split second beforehand what I'm going to say. I draw on everything I've ever had, what I've gathered. And that's probably one force I have. Evidently last Sunday was a good day. They called me up, and I don't know a damn thing I said, because I do not wish to prepare. It has to come from me, where I am, and that's all I am. I work on Sundays. I sit very quietly; I don't eat. I'm not gathering forces. If you want me to tell you where I am, I'm out, over the audience as if I'm looking down on every person. That's my contact of being here. I don't try forcefully to do this; I don't do it by design. Knowing isn't my best force. Not knowing, just *not* knowing, (but knowing) is. Whatever I can draw upon, that is where I am. That is my position. The depth of my knowledge is there. It's stored in a place in my being from where, if I'm honest with the situation, I'll just talk and let it come out. I don't care anymore what comes out. It's not intellectually thought out, or correct. And I'm telling you a secret: This is the way I have to work, and it took me years to get that kind of thing. A hell of a lot of people can't do that, because they haven't got a depth of knowledge. They haven't got a depth of the situation."

"I had a curious idea when I was a boy; it's why I did strange things. I thought, I frankly thought that everything had been expressed. I lived with that for years. And I was just going to say that now. Perhaps someone has already tried this. It took me years and years to get over that idea. In living, we should be able to conquer almost anything."

"For a long time, I couldn't talk at all, I couldn't express an opinion, because I had the screwball idea that I had to organize my whole thought. I had to organize it into a kind of a form in order to produce it until I learned the hard, hard way that this was not true at all for me. Just express my thought—and the hell with what anybody thinks, because, as I stressed to this boy, everybody's in the same boat. No matter what you say, or think, or do, everybody is there. It's on different gradations of understanding, but don't have any fears about talking. I had to get over that, and I have no fears about hurting, insulting, or giving everybody everything I've got. I have no fears about it at all. Either they believe it or not; I don't know; I don't care. They will or they will not. That's the way you have to produce. And, of course, it's impossible."

"I've known this for some time... for anyone to take short-hand of what I have to say, because my sentences are not correct. They're not organized, they're not put into a category of 'he meant this, he meant that.' It can't be done because it's all screwed up. The actual thought is lost. I'm just as glad about that; it's better than what they could write. So I explained to them how to think seriously about their lives and their work and said, 'When you're dead, you're dead for a long, long time.' There is this biblical question in *Solomon,* 'Man should rejoice in his works for that is his portion,' no more, no less. I think that's a marvelous statement. It doesn't matter in what age these things are written; it fits a great deal of the picture today. That's all that you get out of life, what you have done, what you have expressed. No more, no less. That's all. That's your life. And I said, 'Do you want to lead such a life that nothing has happened to you?'"

"With these things in view, if you are to write something of your life's story, you have to remember something of the greater thing that could be than just that, because that's not the shock that I'd like to put forward. The shock would be something that I'm striving toward and for, in a general way, not in my wacky way; because there's no direction in my way, and I don't want any direction. I don't think any good thoughts come in a directed line. They come in a different way; I'm quite certain of that. That's why I'm not against and I'm not for organizations. I'm not for a hierarchy, and I'm not for a group of people who think they are superior, because they are *not*! If they were, I'd say, 'yes,' but they're not."

"There's one line, 'the ancient darkness of the race.' I think that's the most marvelous thing, because that's where it is. It's not with everybody, but it is with many people. And it tells how to forgive them. You have to forgive them, because they don't know what the hell they're doing."

"When you get down to thinking where are we in this little grain of civilization, the great harping on technology and the computer and all the things that are happening to the human race, I wonder what this type of thing is leading to. I cannot be swamped by living in this existence; I cannot afford it. It'd kill me to get caught up in this kind of thing. That's why I retreat here to think things over as deeply as I know how and can. Sometimes I'm in a bad, bad way, and sometimes I'm in a very good way, and most of the time I can remember, and that's a wonderful asset. I'm able to tackle these jobs."

"Then they spoke about Phillis Wheatley and her struggle to have her poetry published. Some 'brain' in this country [Thomas Jefferson] said, 'Well, it's too bad it's so subnormal,' referring to the poetry. The point was it had a terrific impact on the colored people that this person should write poetry. But the man that made this comment… he was some great wit. It wasn't Emerson or anybody, but it was some great, well-known figure at the time, I've forgotten his name. But this colored man on the radio said, 'If they had the education that most of the poets had, and have…' This only came out of their very depths; you understand… and to have it be insulted. It would not have been subnormal, and it wasn't, but he says it would have been wonderful if they'd had an exercise for their brain, the education to do research, look up a word that had ten meanings…."

"I feel like that, like that colored person who was trying, with every part of my being in use, and it's fatal, I know, in many ways, because I'm naive enough to think that people are going to respond honestly, you understand, and people don't."

"Yes, I spoke a little about finding oneself standing in torpor. Do you know what torpor is? You're unable to think, unable to function, just until you break that down. This torpor exists and can easily be taken on by millions of people. It's the shock of a person, or a situation, or a happening that will arouse you, make you become alive and with lifeblood running through your veins, instead of just standing there like death. Then you can act, and that could be the moment of your actual beginning, or anything—that activity that's been thrown at you. You're forced to do it, and if you don't take advantage of it then, you go right back and repeat that situation."

"This is what's happening to a great many of us. We stop thinking, we stop everything, and it's not a question of not caring. We *do* care. When aroused, we do care and as I said before, we can do anything. Mme. de Salzmann is terribly wise and clever, the way she acted with me, understanding just that. In the winter she kept on asking me to come on over to France, because she had something for me to do, without saying what. And you know what it was? When I got there and started talking to these Frenchmen, two hundred or three hundred people…. Now, that is what is known as being taken by surprise, until you're all activity. And by God, at that moment I was absolutely unafraid. And I produced. I would stop, thinking I had said enough, and she said, 'Continue.' And, I tell you, I found myself producing, and that was something wonderful."

"I think in a curious way, people years ago had clever minds, but they were not fast thinkers. This is a crazy theory of mine, because it doesn't happen to me that I can, as I think things through, and start writing it. It's no good. Take a person like Gorham Munson, he was a slow conversationalist. But in that tempo he was able to retain his thoughts and write them out as fast as they happened. Mine are gone when I start writing. I know I have missed some points and I can't retrieve them. So I always thought maybe they're slow enough to express it. It's the most curious thing. I have a good line of thought and when I start writing it, it withers. Not on a big subject, but on emphatic little things. They don't happen that way to me. Like Mr. Gurdjieff wrote this whole goddamn book of millions of words and had the whole thing in mind. And, that's something else again, when you have a big subject in mind, you know you can approach it from many, many angles. But when there's no subject in mind, and then you write little things … the main subject is your own self, your own development. Then you have to write, if your write, something towards that end … but then it's in the wilderness all the time."

"A lot of things have to be done when a person is inspired. And to what end? Not that the end is seen, but they're going towards something. And Orage used to give talks on this kind of thing … about writers … and he said, 'Even constipation will affect people.' Anything … you can tell right down the line—all kinds of things. When my wife was in the hospital, and I was distressed, I could no more think of writing than flying a kite, or putting anything down. It didn't matter. I think the idea of inspiration and if it could be done at that time …. It's not like newspaper reporting where the day is the subject. It's a curious thing with the forms of writing; what do you write for?"

"Why does a person want to write? And there are many, many arguments about that. Of course to affect people, the highest form of writing is scriptural writing, which is done in simple forms. All religious writings are done in simple form. It's the composition that really makes the effect. It's the way the thing is constructed. And the subject is always man's salvation, no matter how you look at it and that kind of affects people. It's affected people for thousands of years. Now we can't go to the highest form of writing, because writing has been reduced to all kinds of things."

"The world will step aside to let a man pass if he knows where he is going. You could delve into everything. It's in the sense of being. Aside from knowledge, one can arrive at a state of being and talk their head off and not know what the hell they said!"

"I understand. I'll ask you to ask yourself. I won't ask you out loud. If it means a child that you're responsible for, your strength will have to be greater. If it means the killing of a human being, your strength will have to be greater. Within the scope of those two things, there isn't anything on earth.... If neither of those things have happened, you'll be able to deal with the situation without making a terror, or else becoming ill. This is one way of becoming ill, when you live within the terror of living instead of its glorification. Whatever has happened to you, you have to realize fully, deeply, *this is my life.* This has happened to *me.* I happen to be here, I happen to be part of this, and this is a part of me.

Once I approached the Old Man when I was suffering tremendously, and he told me exactly those words. And he said, 'You see that skin? That is yours and no one else's. This is a part of you.'"

"One of the curses of civilization is that we have been raised on graciousness and morals. The whole moral question comes up before us, and that can defeat us, like lightning. That is the terror—this whole idea of morals, and refusing to accept the situation that, just like an artist, we live in emotions, by what we have painted. We have great emotional happiness in making that, and we try to relive it. It's just as bad, on the other hand, to continue feeling bad about the situation. All situations are about other people. There's hardly anything about ourselves. There's hardly anything that we go through that's about us. It's always somebody else, something else, some other situation. And we relive it and relive it and relive it. And we do other things."

"I went around the world a couple of times. I was seeking something, and I tried to forget. There's no such thing as forgetting, but you do not have to make it the focal point of your life. That should not be the point of your existence. There should be something greater and greater in order to overcome this."

"I had a hell of a time. I happened to be out at the University of Oregon in a house that was right on the campus. World War II ended, and many of the boys started coming home; some of them got married, some of them got drunk, and some of them didn't know what to do. It got so that I had about fifteen of them at the college—they lived right there at the campus, thinking they'd get over this thing. They all suffered from remorse over the war and the things they had done. They used to gather on the porch, and we talked things over. I had to talk to them as if they were a group, and never, never reveal where I got any of my information, or who I was, or what I was doing. One of them was a sailor who had gone ashore with the invasion of some island. They captured twenty Japanese, and he was put on guard duty, and he killed them all. Just shot them all. Well, he never got over it. Things like that... all kinds of things happened through remorse, complete remorse. I heard that story a thousand times. How could he stop this? How could he stop this line of thought?"

"Until you get to something deeply within yourself where you actually know this can happen, and you start working a little bit—that'll cover a little more time—slowly this other thing, that you do not forget, will take another place. Now, outside of the two things I mentioned, you have the great possibility of overcoming all those things, because the two that I mentioned are the vital things of life and death—two partings of the human race, that you can't get over. That's one of those things. You could, if you're thick skinned enough, but if you're not, and you're really trying, you could."

"Ordinarily our civilization is such that we live under a terrific moral code—not the Scandinavians. In Scandinavia, this kind of thing doesn't exist; they have a wackiness of their own.

For a thousand years they were not civilized and then they were raised in a Calvinistic moral code. If anything can be said to be a curse, this moral code cursed America—the moral code in every township, every hamlet, from coast to coast."

"It's Scotch Calvinism, and these are the people throughout the Midwest that hang you. 'The good people.' I always talk about those 'good people.' They'll kill you by looking at you. Now, if you've gotten that deeply within your veins, you're going to have a hell of a time with it, to break that kind of code in order to live normally and not become sick. Why do you become sick? I never get sick. I hadn't had a cold for about ten or twelve years, then suddenly I got sick, sitting and worrying and with sickness all around me. You become ill, and you can't afford to become ill for too long a time."

"Is this understandable at all? You can overcome it by thinking... by thinking and getting deep down. Now, I will attempt to do this in my way... not somebody else's way, but my way. That is the kind of freedom we can find, if we can find our way, because all of us are different, and all of us are alike. That's my approach. Even Mme de Salzmann has a hell of a time, but she thinks I'm in wonderful shape because I produce my way and not something else, within the range of the Work. I use the Work, but it has to fit me. You cannot 'stylize' everybody and put them into one kind of picture."

"You see, I have this big thing about Armonk that I put my energies and my thought to. I go to be occupied, you know, and to function. And that they can't understand either. And every time there was something, I was always there, because what's the use of having all that property and nobody use it. And it'll never become mellow like a violin or even our harp from lack of use. Except that spot that I know I'm going to occupy down there. That'll have some vibrant ring. But I'm not comparing, I'm just trying to show you that curious thing even with good people—that's why I always say, beware of the good people."

3 | GROWING UP

*"But the stories of early childhood are
very impressive, because I was left wild..."*

"I WENT TO THE EARTH, and I was never forgiven. We had all
these seafaring people. And when I went up to the country,
they couldn't understand that. It was greatly discussed in the
family, never telling me not to do it, but always asking why
didn't I go to sea? So when the war came, my brother went
into the Navy. That was just fine. But I went to the Army.
They said, 'Nothing can be worse than this, that you're doing
this to your family.'"

Who would complain?
"All the old sea captains, because they knew my father. He
was well known, and my mother was always there. They came
up to drink. Jesus Christ, they drank. My mother came over
here when her father packed her off to come over in a sailing
ship with my father when they got married. Everything was
loaded with brandy and Aquavit, and she didn't drink. She'd

look at me every once in a while and she'd say, 'I often wonder what happened to all that brandy and liquor I brought over here?' I said, 'What the hell, look at what you had in the house, all this time.' Well, I had to be nice to them, you know. She didn't drink, and my brother didn't drink, but I drank."

"'Your grandfather,' my mother used to say, speaking of her father, 'had vats of Aquavit, and he went to bed with five vials under his pillow. And at certain hours, he'd take a mouthful and spit it out to see if the vats were working properly.' He could go by taste; these five vials were with him, and he'd wake up right on the dot. That's using the sense of taste, like these men who taste the Vermouth, the wine tasters. They could tell you the place it grows in. One man could tell you the farm it comes from and the row of grapes the damn thing comes from. That's the sense that I'm talking about trying to develop—not only taste, but all your senses."

"After the war, I went up to the Adirondacks and became a lumberjack. Well, Jesus, my family almost died. 'You can't be any lower than a lumberjack. That's the lowest. Lousy lumberjacks.' That's what they all said. And then when I came home, I went to Cranberry Lake for a while, up in Syracuse. I was going to be a forester. But then I decided, 'No, it's no good for me.' I decided the lonely life, the isolated life, was not the thing for me. At that time I was really searching, feeling my way. I didn't want advice. I *needed* advice, but I did every damn thing on my own guts and effort. I have nobody to thank for that, except that I thank my mother for leaving me alone."

"Then, when I saw I should live outside, I decided to become a farmer and went back and told the family, 'I'm going to be a farmer.' Well, they were nonplussed...that was the end of the world. And everyone was always saying, 'What would your father say?' Well, what *would* he say? They never forgave me for not going to sea."

"Of course, I did go to sea. After the war I went to sea for a couple of weeks at a time. And I was sent to sea very young. My mother packed me off. She hated the sea because all the men were killed, but that was the thing to do. The family had some pull; we knew all the sea captains and the port captains of the various companies, and evidently we knew The Standard Oil Company. They got me onto a tanker through the port captain because he knew my father, and I was supposed to rise up within the company. Well, I made a couple of trips to Texas City in Galveston on the tanker. Then I came home and I said, 'I quit. The sea is all right for two or three weeks at a time, but no longer.'"

"Oh, Jesus, what a fight. You have no idea what it was like. You have to imagine. The curious thing is, at that time nobody ever said anything. You could do anything. But over the long term, everybody had a voice...saying that you were going to become 'a lousy farmer.' You were never forgiven for those things. They just couldn't understand what a bastard I was."

"There was one very curious thing about my sister. She more or less raised me, and I became very, very close to her. She knew everything I did. I went to school with her when I was two, and I was a very well behaved kid, always starched in ruffles and a Buster Brown collar, and I had a regular bang haircut. My mother used to cut my golden hair. I sat in the back of the class on a bench and drew pictures; evidently, if you were well behaved, they let you do that. But my sister said she was sitting in the class, trying to hear. The training was good in those days, even though you'd say it was too much for a child. My sister was young as hell. She never took her eyes off me for over two minutes, to see if I was there, and at the same time she was listening and learning. You see, you become acute to certain things. She said, 'Never over two minutes did I not glance over to see you.' Then I'd draw the teacher a picture and just walk up to the teacher to show it because that was the thing to do. I don't remember the teacher, but her name was O'Grady. She was from an Irish immigrant family, and terribly nice, evidently, because she used to come up to consult with my mother about me."

Do you remember the classroom?
"I remember once being there, once. I had gone there for a long, long time. I was well behaved. We were never lectured; we had to sense the thing on our own. I thought, later on, that it made my sister keener and more acute, you know, in her development as a child. You couldn't say that things were taken away from her. This was the life of the times. Children are not put on the spot that much these days. My sister was responsible. She felt her responsibility. This is what responsibility is."

"But I was self-sufficient from the minute I was born, I guess. I'd be on my own. When I was three, that's when I found my park. I walked alone for six or eight blocks and I found this park. I sensed it the way horses smell water. I found this big oak tree, and that was my tree. Once my sister found me there she always knew where to look for me. I'd go there all the time."

"That was my tree. But it was always the natural forces, and I think I was born with that idea. The tree was always in my existence. Somewhere in my sensitivity the tree existed. And even in violent thunderstorms I couldn't understand why my sister would come for me, and we'd have to run into a house. I couldn't understand that. Why not stay under the tree? That always amazed me. This was in Carroll Park, in Brooklyn, I think. I used to just walk there, walk away often. It was probably six or eight blocks away. I went like a bullet to this place. Years ago no one ever stopped children. Now they stop children."

"I remember once she came because a terrible thunderstorm was coming. We were standing outside, in a nice neighborhood, and the people hauled us in. It was one of those downpours. And then, after it stopped, we were soaking wet. We dried off, and they were terribly nice, and we went home. But I remember that. That registered on me."

"All kinds of impressions registered. There are times that can become dangerous. I was supersensitive, and I was sensitive to names. I sang, as a child. I know I had a good voice. I was called 'Martin Caruso,' and I had to live that down … 'There goes Martin Caruso,' they'd say. That is agony. I was so goddamned embarrassed. That's what I mean—sensitivity overcame me. I'd walk blocks out of my way to avoid seeing anybody who knew me."

"There was a boy, years ago in those neighborhoods, with a violin. He suffered, I'll tell you, because you were a sissy if you played the violin. The names, the nicknames, that kids got from one another … sometimes they stuck and sometimes they didn't. I was embarrassed all the time. I was that kind of crazy."

Wasn't there something in your childhood that indicated the direction you would go in?
"Yes. You would think I had followed a pattern, because I almost remember, step by step, as I grew older. School didn't mean a hell of a lot to me; I had been studying quite alone for a long, long time. I was interested in the natural forces, then, and the ocean—I was almost a part of it, from birth, by the family, and I knew all sorts of knots from the captains. I was supposed to go to sea, and they brought up charts for me to look at. I looked at them, and I became fascinated with that idea."

"I was terribly religious, in the sense that I knew something better existed. That's all I knew. I didn't know canon law, the laws of the churches, or anything like that. I used to go to church once in a while, then I'd quit. Nothing obvious. There was one church I went to because they made it of green limestone—it's quarried up here in Vermont or one of the New England states. They made the whole church green, and I liked the look. I just liked the color, I think. So I went in there and discovered they had an organization, like soldiers, for kids, you know some of the schools have cadets. This was in the church, in the Sunday schools. They had this cadet corps in uniform. Many of the Protestant churches had these things."

"That's when I quit. I don't know why, but I just quit. That was one of the reasons. I didn't like the idea of these kids playing soldiers and everybody acting important. I was so goddamned sensitive to that—that this was no good. I steered clear of all that kind of thing."

"But my reading was the great issue. In a curious way, the only reason why I should have gone to a school or college or something was for reference. I had to be my own reference. I had to sense what I had to read. College would guide you in certain ways, but I guided myself. Then I went off the deep end about many, many things, as I do today about geology, the ice age, and such things. I became fascinated with these things—I'm interested in the most peculiar things that nobody would be interested in. That's the way I've always, always been—in search, in search of something."

"Christ, what I didn't go through. Then I retreated. I went up to the mountains, and lived in this log cabin. I was about fifteen. I told my mother; I was allowed to do anything."

"There used to be a shop on Chambers Street called Shoveling, Daley and Gale's. They had goods in there, moccasin shoes and things that you have never seen. I had mine for years and years and years. They lasted forever. I could buy all kinds of footwear and warm clothes. My mother packed them, and I went up to the country. I lugged most of the stuff for eight miles."

But you had a very sane childhood...?
"Mine was sane because for Scandinavians, it was given that we had to work. I had to get the firewood, so I would bring boxes from the grocery store, and I'd steal a lot of wood from a building that was in progress and chop it up. And I enjoyed it. It was my job. I had tons of wood for two coal stoves, and it was my job no matter what the hell happened."

"Once they cut down a big tree somewhere nearby, and I went down to get the wood. I never worked so hard in all my life, getting logs from the thing. And it was no good... all green and heavy as hell. But I slaved over these darned things. It must have been an elm. I don't remember; I was about nine or ten years old. But it must have been an elm because you couldn't split the damn thing."

"Things like that were wonderful. Normal. You never talk about dangers that you've been in. Every day you were in danger of something. You never say a word about that so there wasn't any great correction. One time I fell overboard, into the East River, and came home soaking wet. I don't know how I fell over. There was about forty feet of water there, but I could swim enough to get out."

Did you fall over from that boat you used to get into?
"The ferry... that was a different thing. We didn't fall; we sank. That was the thrill. Nobody worried about a goddamn

soul. It was so overcrowded. It was probably only a few inches out of the water, with all the kids in it. We would hide in back of the pier and then when the ferryboat pulled out, we'd row like hell in back of it to get into the waves. Big high waves, you know, from the side-wheelers. We'd go up and dive down and sink. Everybody was in amazement there, you know, on the ferryboat. We were all kids."

How old were you then?
"I was very young. We were all kids. But we had a freedom that never exists now. In Scandinavia, the kids in the water come down and see the little boat run on the Göta Canal going across Sweden. They'd see the little boat coming, right up close to the towns, and the kids running down the street would see the boat and jump overboard, with all their clothes on, yelling and screaming. No fences or anything. Well, that's freedom. Nobody worried about them. They had to learn how to swim."

"Then we'd go fishing for crabs, catching crabs with a scalping net. We lost so many nets, because the kids would see a crab and get excited and fall overboard. But we used to catch a hell of a mess of crabs in the harbor and off the piers. And then, every seven years there was a little fish like a small silvery flounder about a foot long, called a lafayette. The lafayettes used to run every seven years. You could throw a line in, with three or four hooks, and pull up three or four fish. We used to get tons of fish. Jesus, what a sight! The water was just full of lafayettes. That was a terribly enjoyable thing."

"And we didn't have much of anything. Nobody had a boat. We made rafts. And boy, it was worth your life if you ever got out far enough, because there was the current going out, and the damn rafts used to turn around in the currents. Then there was Buttermilk Channel, between Governor's Island and Brooklyn Heights. It's a swift-flowing current there. Just before we got into the Second World War the battleship *Missouri* went down Buttermilk Channel, and they grounded. Instead of going out around Governor's Island on the outside or the inner rim—you know, the regular route—they went on the other side, and they got grounded. They had to take off the guns, they had to unload the ammunition, take off all the weight."

That's where you played as a kid?
"Yes. It was a wild current. It was a narrower place than the other side, which had the whole harbor, you see. My brother used to swim to Governor's Island and back. I never did that, but he was a powerful swimmer. You had to get miles down and go with the current and try to make it. If you didn't make it, you'd go right down the East River. There was excitement all the time as children—not afraid of a damn thing."

"I had wonderful observation as a child. There was an idiot on each block. We had one, and we used to call him Dumont. He was deaf and dumb. Dumont went with the gang, but he didn't know what was happening. We had to guide him. Then there was an idiot whom everybody fed, and then there was an orphan. Every street had these two or three things. Poor isolated kids… but they grew up healthier and more normal than most children today. The orphan boy was Angelo Benedetto. He was Italian, very dark and very husky. My mother used to give him my clothes. He slept in cellars, and we used to 'capture' a grocery wagon every Saturday and push it down into that basement, and that was his food for the week. We didn't know what the hell was in it — we'd steal it, and get the thing unloaded, and take it out and push it down the street. They knew, but they didn't know. And we didn't ever know what was in the thing."

"One time we had Angelo water our garden. We had a yard, and watered the flowers and things. There was a woman next door who was very English and mean as the devil to all of us wild kids. Angelo squirted the hose on her over the fence, and she went up and reported him to the police. That is all you had to do. And his name was put on the book. Nobody knew about this until he went through the school. And then he studied. He didn't go through high school because that was impossible there, but he studied enough to become a fireman. But before they'd clear him as a fireman, this was against him. So he had to go around and find us and we sent letters in, and got him on as a fireman."

"Then he studied like hell, and suddenly he became a lieutenant, and we thought that was wonderful. He used to come out to see us all the time. He didn't have any family. Then he got married to a terribly nice person, I think my sister knew her. And then he became captain. And he rose right up in the ranks until he became marshal of the fire department. He was captain of Staten Island, then of Brooklyn, and then of someplace else, and then he became marshal. These kids were more normal. Their minds were clearer. The life was tough. It was hard living, but that helped them a great, great deal. It didn't hinder them."

"Angelo had a wonderful little boy. They used to come to Staten Island, and he would go out by himself, this little fellow, and he'd come back and say, in all seriousness, 'I just saw a bear. He's right there, right in back of those two trees. Now, you watch.' He saw that bear, no matter what. Well, I loved that. The kids used to see all kinds of things. It's more than imagination—I think he *did* see the bear."

"Kids all fight. Boys fight like hell. The only disturbance we ever had was when the fathers came down to raise hell. One father chased me for miles, I think, and I ran like hell, because I beat up his son. I don't know what for. I got away and I just ran. That was just creeping in then, families protecting their children. Now you'll get arrested if they start fighting. It was normal living, in the sense that you had to struggle."

"Every day was a struggle. We used to try to collect junk in order to get a few pennies. One time we stole a railroad track. Not the whole track, you couldn't carry it, but we stole a big piece. All the kids got on it and moved it into the lot, and then we picked it up—it was heavy as hell—and we'd sell it piecemeal. We would get twenty cents or forty cents that had to be divided up among all of us. Then there was the banana boat—one of those things you don't see anymore. We'd all go down to the banana boat to get bananas because they threw a lot of them away when they were ripe. The Italian laborers carried one big stalk. When a ripe one came they'd give all the kids that stood around, like kids in Haiti, bunches of bananas for free. But that was all right. We weren't raiding anything."

"Then there was the ice. The ice industry was very important for the whole civilization along the Eastern seaboard. Ice was shipped to Charleston from New York harbor and the ice boats would come, ten or twelve at a time, through the Erie Canal and down. I made a two-wheeled wagon so that the wheels would balance. I made a square shaft that would fit into it. And I'd go down on Saturday and get ten cents worth of ice, which was more or less a whole cake and which was all I could pull, and then sell pieces of it. You only got five or ten cents, and you had to lug it upstairs and put it in the iceboxes, but anything to get five or ten cents. That was our spending money. Sometimes on a Sunday, if we were very good, we'd get a nickel for a soda. That's all … a nickel. And that soda … my God! How we'd work over that!"

"But all these curious things, the recollections of early childhood … the world will never see that age again. Everything was expensive because you didn't have a penny. You never had anything. We had a couple of pennies, but things were cheap as dirt."

"At that time they still used a great deal of British words, like I would be sent to the grocer for a shilling's worth of eggs. That was the term, 'a shilling's worth of eggs.' Then we had the term 'a baker's dozen,' which was thirteen. When you went to the meat market you got a slice of liverwurst or baloney from the butcher. He'd get calves in and carry them cheap as … God! how they could carry that stuff! Whole calves with their fur on them, their skins. I wanted one of those skins to cover my sled and the butcher promised me a skin for a hell of a long time. Finally he gave me one, and I tacked it on my sled—that way I could go belly whopping down the street."

"There was excitement all the time. The people were pretty close to one another; everybody knew every damn thing about everybody else. There were no secrets. We had an Irish family named Kelly. They had a daughter named Bella, and the mother was very sick, dying of tuberculosis. She had two boys, Jean, and another daughter. He had a beautiful voice. Then the First World War came, and I heard that he was singing in all the vaudeville shows, singing "The Star Spangled Banner." He had a high tenor natural voice. I had a good voice, but he went on with his. But then he started drinking. I met him many years later and I said, 'What the hell happened?'"

"Well, he lived with his sister, Jennie. Jennie was a schoolteacher. But then there was a cousin, who lived across the street. She was named Kathleen Marr. Isn't that a wonderful name? And Kathleen was a street-walker. She was so beautiful … I think most of the kids were raped by Kathleen Marr. I guess she went with men since she was fourteen. It was a shame about Kathleen. She finally died, according to Jean."

"And the curious thing is, he used to tell us that when his mother was sick and dying, she was always beating him up.

His father would hold him by the bed when she wanted to beat him up, while she switched hell out of him with a stick. A dying woman—I never heard of such a thing. He was beaten up, this poor kid. No wonder he took to drink. The father was a real Irish, crazy Irish, and the mother was, too. I never saw that happen. We were never beaten up in our family at all. My mother used to hit me with a newspaper once in a while, and that was all I ever got. But we were pretty well-behaved kids."

Well, how did your mother keep you in line?
"Oh, she was working all the time. We were pretty good. I was wild as hell. I think, in a sense, I missed my father. We had no guidance from a man. My brother was nine years older—he was studying like hell; and I was the hell-raiser of the family. I did everything.... Oh, there were all kinds of predictions: 'This and that's going to happen to you.'"

Who said that?
"My brother. He was so much older, nine years older. It's a helluva distance. When I was very young, I used to stay out with the kids talking on the street and playing basketball. That was coming to the poorer areas. We'd put barrel hoops on a lamppost and play half the damn night. You know what a black raincoat looks like? You could buy a black football. It was made in sections, and you got a key, and you blew it up. It cost about a quarter and you played football with them. We'd all have to chip in to pay for the football. But they were

strong. And, oh! How we ran, until we were ready to collapse and just drop dead."

"You would see kids selling ice cream—little kids, at the bridges and everything, during the Depression. But we weren't sent out for money, my God."

"The big thrill was to see Christy Mathewson pitch. He had tuberculosis, but he pitched no-hitter games. Christy Mathewson was just a withered creature from the tuberculosis. We wanted to see him, and we'd raid the place, a gang of us, and slip right in like eels. Right away you had to learn tricks: get in there and turn and look pious as hell. Kids do such things. Anything they had a will to do it; they would surely do it."

"I was down around the Battery a great deal as a kid, because there was excitement—the ships coming in and all. There were a lot of sailing ships then. The immigrants, just released and coming in from Ellis Island, had big pads on them, and everything they owned was in big trunks and tied up, and they couldn't speak a word of English."

"I swear, the kids years ago, no matter what language they were speaking, you could get to the tonal quality of their speech and understand them, and figure out where they wanted to go. We would direct them. It was a wonderful lesson for kids. We were thrown right into the middle of a wave of foreigners who we got to know."

"Then would come Christmas. My mother used to work with lutfisk for six weeks. It is that flat fish that you see off the cliffs in Norway and Sweden. You dry them, and they're cut, and you soak them in every damn thing to pull them back out to their real sizes. Then we made what they call 'schweiner sylte'—headcheese from pigs' heads. My mother would buy a pig's head, and I would have to get the butter tub, and then when the pig's head was cooked, she would take the skin off, put cheesecloth in the butter tub and then line that inside with the skin. Then she added particles of meat until you got a big lump, and then you twisted the cheesecloth and put a weight on it—a heavy weight, boards and weight, until it would come out round and compressed. Then it was allowed to stand for weeks, solid, like that, and it held together. Then there were all the cookies—Jesus, what cookies. And all the bread made for Christmas. Oh, it's a great feast. Christmas Eve we had to eat the fish and rice. There was a whole ceremony and then Aquavit and everything. We all drank. My God, it was a Scandinavian household."

Who all would come on Christmas Eve, besides immediate family?

"Captains and such, because they knew my mother would cook all this stuff and get it all ready. There was a Tom Thompson who was one of the strongest men, I think, in existence. We called him Uncle Tom. He was Norwegian, big and powerful, and he went in for a tug-o'-war."

"Did you know they had professional tug-o'-wars? New York had a team, and Chicago had a team. All the different cities had tug-o'-war teams, and he was the anchorman. This big rope would stretch, and he had to take the loop around his waist. Professional tug-o'-war and they'd get set with cleats and everything. And these powerful men…But you'd see the rope stretch. And everyone…They had a flag. They'd get set and then shoot a pistol or something, and the tug-o'-war was on. The team that he was on would win all the time. We weren't allowed to go, but my brother went; and he told us Tom Thompson's veins used to stick out from the pressure. And he'd come over on Christmas."

"My sister said I locked myself in a room as a child, when I was two or three years old, and I couldn't get out. They were trying to tell me how to turn the key, but I couldn't turn that goddamned key. I did everything but turn it. And I started to yell, I guess. I didn't know what the excitement was. This was up on the second floor."

"Then Tom Thompson climbed the face of that building, and he came in one window and out the other and swung over. We haven't got men like that, I'll tell you. Not afraid of a damn thing—he swung in there, got the window open, and got me out."

"As children, we made chains of decoration for the tree. We made all the decorations: Objects and chains and things and cookies."

"But the tree business was something—to get that Christmas tree, without buying a tree. They had tons of trees. They came by boat and came by train and everything. We'd wait until Christmas Eve because they'd have to get rid of the trees. The family would band together, my sister and brother and me—it took a family to get a tree. Then the man, who was always enraged that he didn't sell all the trees (they still don't) would throw them, brutally throw them at the kids. If you were with your family, you grabbed that tree. You fought like a tiger for that damned tree. If you had hold of a Christmas tree it would be like a lion or a tiger with her cubs. You'd fight the devil himself for that tree. No one dared come near you. That was your tree. You fought for it and won it. And that's how we got our trees. But what a struggle. That was the struggle that was hard and tough, and no one expected any other treatment than that. We had no rights."

"That was the way we got a Christmas tree. You learned something doing that kind of thing: not only survival but what you had to get, by God, you got it...It was like going to war. My brother was very strong. I wasn't as strong, but he was physically strong, and my father was a strong person too. Husky. I was never powerful like that. I was always a skinny runt.

"When I was about ten years old, there was a police station. The police station was locked, with a wooden fence around it. It didn't cover half a block, but it covered about a third of it. And there was a white horse grazing in the yard. This white horse and I became very friendly, because I always loved animals. So we'd jump over the fence and we were very friendly with the horse. We were frightened, but not frightened. We made friends with the horse and he knew that we wouldn't harm him."

"They had bicycle policemen in those days, who wore knickerbockers and black stockings. And there was this cop, who we always thought was a real bastard. His name was—I'll never forget—Nat Pendleton. He was a neighborhood person. He knew all the kids, and he knew the families. But he rode this bicycle. That was his job. We didn't know, but all the cops were chasing kids. He saw that we were in this field, so he started chasing us, and yelling over the fence, and we'd run to the other side, and he'd race around, and we'd run back. And finally, he jumped over the fence, and the horse chased him. I'll never forget that: this big white horse went after him and grabbed him on the shoulder. So we jumped over the fence. And he was always out for revenge on poor kids who hadn't done anything. That was our fault for a hell of a long time."

"Years ago, certain houses had dumbwaiters, to send your groceries up or your garbage down. There was one house where we knew there was a dumbwaiter, because it was a new house. We saw it being made, so before anybody moved into the damn house, we started pulling one another up and down in this dumbwaiter. And that was something, yelling and screaming with the counterweight coming down full speed—that was a real danger, I'll tell you. You could have been pulled right up with the damn thing. We played with that for weeks before they got wise to us, and we were chased out of there."

"This was in a nearby place. I don't remember where the hell it was. You see, there was civilization where we lived, but all of Brooklyn was a cabbage patch. All of Bensonhurst... there wasn't a house for miles. Then came the migration. You could see it from the streetcar—the migration of Italians who planted little gardens and cabbage patches all over the damned place. Now it's all gangsters and slums. It'll go back to the earth, you know, soon."

"We had tough times. My sister must have had brittle bones. We were involved in hospitals, mostly on account of her. And my God, I have to knock on wood, I never got a broken bone. I got stitches in my hand; you can see where I'm all cut to ribbons. Somebody was stealing my roller skates from the basement, and I heard it and I ran down into the basement, and the thief ran out and slammed the door, a plate glass door, and I got cut. I caught up with him and started knocking the stuffing out of him. I thought I was killing him because of all the blood. My mother saw me and she said, 'What in the world are you bleeding from?' I didn't know I was cut, so I was marched upstairs. I had to go to the hospital to get stitched up."

"But my sister…my mother showed great courage with her. She had a tough, tough life, especially with the whole family—my father who died, my sister who died, and then my other sister with the broken arms and legs. You were desperate when you were in that situation. I'll never forget when my sister told me that my mother told the hospital, 'Any legs to be cut off, I cut them off, not you.'"

"So she took my sister and put her in my baby carriage, and got a young surgeon and said, 'Now you listen to me.' And she told him the story of how they neglected her and gangrene set in. They were going to cut her leg off. My mother went up there and carried my sister off. They sent two policemen to arrest the whole damn family because they wanted to perform this operation. That's the only thing they knew—how to cut arms and legs off. My mother said, 'No.' They performed the operation on the kitchen table, and my mother gave the chloroform to my sister and everything. She lost two small bones in her leg, but they more or less scraped the gangrene off, and she said, 'We'll put her in a plaster cast.' Because my mother knew that during the Civil War they ran out of plaster and bandages took over, and the poor soldiers suffered like hell every time they removed these bandages. My mother knew these things from her mother who was a doctor. They put bandages on my sister's legs, of course, but they made a plaster cast over the legs."

"Then we had to go to court, and when my sister testified she was fortified by my mother. My mother got up there to fight the world. All the doctors of the hospital called the whole family liars, and said that it wasn't true. They almost had the poor doctor fired from the medical society because they thought he had performed a radical operation. Can you imagine? And my mother had to plead for his sake. She was active as a nurse during the time of the Panama Canal. The government wanted her to go down to handle the Yellow Fever."

"I remember one tough, tough winter. My mother would bundle me up, and I'd go with a can to get some milk. I had woolen mittens and a shawl that she would criss-cross in front of me and then tie around me. That I remember very clearly, and also wandering out into these great snow piles. My mother watched me from the window. I would fall over these snow piles to get across the street to get way down to some little grocery store, then back and fall down again, and return without a drop of milk. I reeled over these things. But I had the can in my hands and nothing else. I would never let go of that can. That never bothered anybody. I didn't know any better. It had a cover on it. It had all gone out. This I remember very vividly. And of course you live for years and years, and you don't remember what the hell happened."

That was because your mother had to work all day?
"Yes. My sister raised me. That was a strange existence. And there wasn't a question of day care and child-care centers. In those days nothing like day care existed. A family unit was on its own, and you were at the mercy of every goddamn thing. We all had chores, and of course one of these things was cleaning. One of my chores was to clean all the carpets on Saturday."

"I raised canary birds, and my sister helped me. I had thirty-two canary birds. Some were crippled and some were normal, but the law of the family was that if you had an animal, you took care of him and I had to take care of these birds. All Saturday and every evening I had to fuss with cleaning the cages. I'll never forget all these canary birds that we had—with a cat who was crazy. Did I tell you about the crazy cat?"

"We had a cat, Minnie, that I swear was crazy, and we had to always watch the canary birds on account of the cat. As soon as you heard the canary birds singing like hell, you knew they were in danger. I'll never forget that cat. I think she was crazy and playful all at once. She loved to frighten strangers. Whenever the doorbell rang, this damn cat knew someone was coming, and would race to my mother's ironing board and sit on top of it, and as soon as the door opened, she'd jump to the top of the door and drop on the person. Everybody almost dropped dead right at the door. It was like a protection—you have no idea. This doctor—a famous doctor—came, and he swore hell out of the cat for dropping on his shoulder. Minnie used to drop on everybody. We were used to it."

"That was when we almost moved back to Sweden. We were living on Henry Street, and I had just been born. The Spanish-American war was going on. I guess it was around the time that we heard that the men were killed. Anyhow, a gang was chasing a young boy, about fifteen, a cabin boy from the ship. A whole gang was chasing him because he was Spanish, and he came running up the street. My mother went out and grabbed him and pulled him into the house, and they broke all the windows in the house. They were going to lynch him. He could have been a Puerto Rican; he could have been from anyplace in South America. That's how vicious the line is still within us. Not from the Middle Ages but way, way back. My mother said, 'I think we'll move back to Sweden. This is an un-civilized country.' And we almost did. She could not imagine this lynching. She'd have protected him with our lives and her own. This wasn't too long ago, and this is still with us."

4 | *S H O C K S*

"You will never know until you are
put on the spot and express yourself."

"IF YOU DON'T DO ANYTHING, it's worse. If you're not going to expose yourself to the shocks that you'll get, nothing will ever happen to you. You won't have to struggle and that struggle may be the best thing in the world for you, instead of leading an insipid life where nothing is going to happen, because you won't take a chance on it. God knows. I know that kind of subject."

"You can walk out of your life, you know, and until you are aroused and shocked—and I've said this a million times—you're unable to come to many, many things until you're shocked into them, aroused into them."

"You all talk about attention, but you haven't got the power to come to a real attention, just by yourself. Most of our existence is through shock. Then we say, 'Well, I did it.' But believe me, it's not your own steam. It's not your own pressure. If you're within this scope and feeling and atmosphere of coming to attention, you'll find that your nothingness, or the void, exists, and not knowing what, or where, or how, or anything. I'm listening to people say they do this, and they do that, and I said, 'When the shock comes, when this thing comes and you're in that atmosphere, that shock has the possibility of doing that to you wherein a catalyst is formed. And between these two pressures, one with all your knowledge and being and the other, with the shock as in, oh, some great happening….'"

"I'm not great enough to give shocks, but it could be any kind of shock, a big shock, so that you'll freeze all the way through, and you may come to the answer. That is the most vital thing in your life, that's the answer. More than thinking it out, more than using your intelligence or your mind—it's within your whole system, and this is your beginning. Then you know what to do. Is that understandable? I'm giving you a big piece of advice of our particular work. We're not capable. We're not weak, but we're not capable until there's a hell of a big shock—a big shock that'll come and hit us and throw us right off the balance, and within that could be the answer. That's the most vital thing that's happening within your life."

"What is that thing they always talk about—attention? I could almost answer that nobody, sitting in a quiet time, can come to attention. You have to be in a receptive part of attention, and it takes a big shock so that you're ready to receive it; that will put you into real attention. Now, you may not believe this, but this is what I have come to. The Old Man was capable of giving us the shock."

"I knew three Frenchmen who were in the worst concentration prison camps in the war, and they had withered to nothing until there wasn't anything left of their whole beings. Even this life didn't matter. And suddenly they came to what we call 'illumination.' They saw the whole picture because the shock was so great in these prison camps. Three of them, in different places, going through that experience and with their emaciated bodies—nothing, just living flesh and bones—they came to this and understood one hell of a lot. Then it leaves them. We call them the lost people. They are lost forever because they always try to get back. They join our Work, they do everything to get back to that position, because they don't know how they got there."

"We know how we're getting there, step by step by step. We can retrieve our steps, but we'll never get where they got. These Frenchmen were cursed forever, trying to get back into this great state that they found themselves in, not knowing how they got there. That's not what we're seeking. I think, in the ultimate end, we'll never, just by virtue of being human beings, reach such a state of consciousness. But we can reach a state of being, a great state of being—to be, alive, on this earth."

"That's what I'm talking about—shocks that you will keep forever and a day. Even though you forget them over the course of years, they are yours and so you can recall them. Now, there's so much to be said about how wrong things are, and there's so much to be said about how right things are. I think the right thing is that we have something; we have a hold of something. I feel this very, very deeply within me. It's not just weaving the words and making trips to France. We have a hold of something that has affected us enough to say, 'This is it.'"

"I'm on a kind of trail where I want to make my own expression, without anybody knowing it. Nobody would know it. Now, see what that does. That's what I have advised you to do with your question. Don't stay on a traditional line of different sects and groups too long; you'll get mixed up, sure as hell. Find out what is in that."

"I tried to tell Bill Segal, [when he was badly injured in a car accident] 'you go to a slaughterhouse for Christ's sake; all that blood-letting. You try to take in these emanations. And in the course of time, with everything you know and the turmoil of you getting well, there could be emanations from you. You've heard everything; possibly you've read everything. And now you have the possibility of making something of everything, because you're immobile. You cannot move. And we'll never put ourselves into that situation.' I said, 'You're lucky that you're like this.' I feel absolutely right in saying this. I feel absolutely that this is the right thing. And I remind him of this."

"I told him, 'Now, don't be like Ivan Osokin who slowly and slowly lost his memory of who he was. You can go the other way. See, you'll have the possibility of making something from this great shock, even through great suffering.' We won't put ourselves in the position of giving ourselves a shock like that, or we just forget. The power of forgetting, I think, is the curse of mankind. I told him, 'Go up to the country. Go up to your place' (they have a beautiful place up in Chester) 'and stay there. Have people build a bunk where you can look at your fireplace. Don't try stairs. Just stay there and have a fire going. And have them serve you something.' And he did that. I said, 'Have them wheel you around and enjoy the existence of the natural forces.' And he called up and said, 'I had the most marvelous day up there in Chester. They fixed me a bed in the living room. It was wonderful to see the fire.' You see, it'll give him new life if he stays with the natural forces of the ordinary things, before he can come to something extraordinary. But he has the possibilities. I have to struggle, my God, because I'm not shocked. I am shocked by conditions, but I'm not shocked the way he is. Like the Old Man was shocked, and almost facing death all the time."

"I know I come to many answers of what I have to do at the ice house. The problems can't be solved, and suddenly in a dream I'll come to the answer, and wake up like that, and there it is. Now, why haven't I thought of it? Or you may trip on a curbstone and come to what must be done. For me to tell you is not possible. It has to hit you, and it has to be a kind of a shock that you will have to get in order to come to it yourself. Desiring it has to be a catalyst, it has to be like that. And once that has jelled, there it is! And that's the answer to your beginning."

"No, no, I tell you I knew this little secret. Years ago when I was at Mendham, I had planted about two and half acres of cabbages. We had a drought somehow and these cabbages came up just like that [*indicates size of an apple*]. And I had a big crew of men one time and I said, 'We make a circle around each plant and have it trenched about three inches.' And we had a big cistern in the barn of liquid manure. And we dragged these big cans out on stone boats and we filled each trench with liquid. Well you've never seen such a crop of cabbages in all your life; I had cabbages like this [*indicating large sized cabbage head*]. They were just waiting for an element—something. And we had a tremendous storage of cabbages, hanging. We did it twice because we had a drought. But that is waiting, just waiting for that one thing. And this is my argument that it is not love. It was waiting for something that it needed so desperately it couldn't live. That's what the Sahara needs—water and the seed will come forth. Everybody thinks the desert is dead and it isn't. It's just waiting to bloom."

Mr. Benson takes a group meeting for Mrs. Benson who is ill. "I can see we have these three laws: the law of three, the law of seven, and the law of nine. It fits into the picture regarding many, many things, even the cosmos. How many planets are there? Nine. This is what Mr. Gurdjieff called 'immutable laws' that guide us in the maelstrom of our lives. Now, I don't teach, but I tell anecdotes, I tell of conditions, and I tell what I believe in, in order to strike my center. This is the message that I wish to put across to you. Seek that more than anything else, because that is yours, your development, your process—that's *you*, and nobody can take that away from you. Now seek again the position to do that. And as it says in the book of *Solomon*, 'Man should rejoice in his works, for that is his portion.' Do you all understand that? No more, no less. That's what you leave behind, that's your development, that's you. Is that understandable?"

"The work with which we're concerned happens to be our Work. We happen to be involved in it together. And there is one theme that is quite true among all of us. We happen to be here, and we happen to be thinking of this work, and how we can do better, through all the gyrations of mankind within the framework of this work. So I would like to go from there, from that picture."

"I have fairly good judgment. As you talk, that's the way you are, in the position of yourself. Not to satisfy me, but for you, and not to satisfy but to find out. I want to warn everyone: you do not know who you are in yourself, in your development, until many factors come up; your studies, your development, your studies towards your growth, towards knowledge... *the sense of being*. To *be* is the one really major factor of your existence, but to get there is a long travail."

"The body disintegrates. All kinds of things happen. But what you have developed into—that is your work—and man should rejoice in his works, for that is his portion. You can't go beyond that because you don't know any better, because you have not yet worked hard and diligently towards something beyond. It works both ways. But to be on the spot, as I am, say, tonight, and because I am ill—it's worse than you think—it's the crazy things I say all the time: I'm worse and I'm better at the same time, because I know this position of being on the spot."

"Hot or cold, no matter what happens, I would be here talking to you all. I can make any excuse in the world. That's where your nerves are on tenterhooks, like that. Everything is out like antennae—you're receiving, and at the same time, by virtue of you all being here, there is a definite force of people. You are receiving another food for the challenge to express your truth. Deep down inside, you make that expression."

"I've said this a thousand times: this is our Work. As I express myself now, that is where I am. Being put on the spot is the best position to be in, and you can't just walk out of the situation and everything you have been seeking all these years. You have a sentence, a word, whole ideas that are never expressed, but through this force you can call it."

"You cannot put yourself on the spot—you have not got the force. Some great happening has to occur, something that affects you, because otherwise you will make every kind of excuse, thinking you know better."

"It's very difficult for me to arouse people to work, to make them sense that this is their life, their only life, and seek. You will never know until you are put on the spot and express yourself. You can mull it over in your mind and produce something, but you don't know. This is the only way I know of, sincerely, deeply— how to Work is to grow."

5 | *THE WAR*

*"No, I didn't enlist through any glorification;
I was just wild, wanted something."*

" WE WERE LIVING IN NEW YORK. I knew of the Army ... or did I?
I guess I did. I went to Whitehall Street, to the army headquarters, because they didn't have recruiting around. You went
there. I was sent to Fort Slocum right away. You enlisted and
you went. Then I came home. That was in 1917. I came home
for Thanksgiving with half a uniform. They didn't have any
uniforms. I had an overcoat and a hat and leggings, or something like that, but no real uniform. Then we were shipped
from Fort Slocum to Fort Meyer, Virginia, and from there we
went to Fort Belvoir, which is very close. And God, we froze
to death. That was the coldest winter on record, 1917. We got
Civil War capes. That was something—the only warm thing
in the whole damn war."

"We slept in shelter tents, outside. But we were all healthy
and strong as hell. Everybody! No rules or regulations—how
to keep alive was the main thing. And I never saw home again.

We marched to Washington. It was one o'clock in the morning, and a hell of a big snowstorm. Right in front of the capitol we marched, and not a living soul saw us. Fifteen hundred of us, and we marched to the railroad tracks, and got on cold Pennsylvania Railroad cars that were frozen. It was bitter cold, about twelve below; it was fifteen below in Hoboken when we arrived there at night, frozen to the hilt, and checked our unit. You'd give your number and then they'd say your name, and you'd give your number, then they'd check you off as legitimate."

"We got on the transport, the old Hamburg America line. The damn thing leaked. We were way the hell down in the bottom, and the porthole leaked. There was about six inches of water on the floor. Canteens, everything went swishing all night. All across, back and forth. Oh my God, nobody slept. And then suddenly, after one or two days, we were in the gulfstream, out of the cold. The gulfstream is warm. It's really hot. And there we were on deck taking showers. Well, that felt wonderful. So we stayed out on deck and the hell with going down below. That was a holy mess. We had our rifles, Springfield rifles, and we had to rescue them, because we were going to war. We were all kids, crazy as hell."

What made you enlist?
"No particular thing. I heard from N.Y. State, from a close friend of mine who was in charge of forestry or parks or some damn thing, named C. R. Pettys. He wrote. He knew I was a wild kid up in the Ramapos, and he said, 'Now, if you have the education and the schooling, I'll see that you get to West

Point.' Well, I didn't have the schooling and education to pass trigonometry and calculus and things like that. I never was a mathematics bug like my brother was. He didn't read, but he became a famous engineer. I wrote back and said, 'I wouldn't think of that kind of thing.' They were actually looking for people to go to West Point at one time. But at the time you could enlist into anything you wished."

"So I thought it over, and I enlisted in the Pioneer Infantry. That was a comeback. It wasn't infantry. I disliked the idea of drilling all the time. You understand? That's all the infantry did was drill. So I said Pioneer Infantry. Pioneer Infantry was like the Sea Bees, who are working sailors and combat engineers where they're in combat all the time, except they're supposed to know this, that and the other thing. Nobody knew a goddamn thing, and it didn't matter. Anybody up front was up front, no matter what they were. You got hit with the same shells, same gas and things. No, I didn't enlist through any glorification; I was just wild, wanted something."

"I was with the first hundred thousand, with no preparation. I was in the army six weeks when I came under shellfire. That was Châlonsby. We got there, stayed at the Napoleon Barracks. Got lice for the first time in Brest. I took the train up to the front from there. We were all kids, and didn't know a goddamn thing about what to do. I didn't know where the hell I was. I brought a loaf of bread in case I was going to starve. Big wheel, you know? And we chipped in."

"That was the first place I got drunk, on account of the lice. It was in back of a fourteen foot wall. These old Napoleon barracks had iron kettles that you had to use. All the cooking was done outside, in the open fires, and we had no wood. The captain said, 'We won't eat tomorrow unless you get wood.' That meant jump the wall and get wood. But I saw a shanty in the early, early morning the first morning we were there. I saw this damn shanty, and I said to our squad—we were scattered all over the place looking—'Let's tear it down.' We tore it down and got arrested by the French infantry and got put in jail, in the dungeon, right at the entrance gate. You could see the grill, and we lived on French soup for a couple of days."

"There were eight of us in the dungeon. One day I heard the voice of the lieutenant, a voice I knew, and we started yelling like hell. They thought we'd deserted. I said, 'We didn't desert, we were arrested.' But they never reported where we were. The lieutenant got us out right away, and the next day we left for the front in boxcars. That was my introduction to France, coming into France. Jesus, what a crazy life. Lousy all the time. But the first night we were there, we had an old hobo named Skelly—he came from Cohoes, New York—who I'll never forget. Never."

"He always talked about Cohoes. He was red-haired and half bald. He was a former marine. He knew all about everything, and he was drunk all during the war, never sober. He was in the guardhouse all the time. So he told all the kids, 'I'll jump the wall—you boost me over and I'll go to town, but I have to have some money.' We all chipped in, and he came back with six bottles of Cognac, on strings. He'd been in the Philippines and Christ knows, everyplace. And he knew the ropes of Army life. He got into our company, God knows how. That's when we all got drunk for the first time and the first night, in France, on account of the lice. It was lousy since Napoleon's day or before."

"Oh, Christ, what a mess, we thought we were in hell. We were furious as hell and had rats all over, this big. So we got out of there, thank God—what a terrible place. We got up to the front, and everyone went out, and they said, 'Follow the Frenchmen.' We were with the French Army you know. We couldn't find any Frenchmen at all, so we found a French canteen. So when everything went out, shells flying all over hell, everybody piled in there and got tight—because they had wine. We stole everything they had—you know, when you're at war you steal anything, and we didn't care. We only got eleven dollars a month. I lived on eleven dollars a month. We got a dollar a day, but I sent fifteen dollars home, and then there was so much, four or five dollars for the insurance. I lost all that goddamned insurance I paid for a couple of years. So I got eleven dollars out of the whole salary."

"Then came a big to-do out of some wackiness I had done—all kinds of crazy things. I was always active because we were always wound up as children to be active. I came upon a whole mess of Belgian refugees living in holes in the ground right beside the Marne River. They were living in complete squalor and poverty, men, women and children. I felt so damned sorry for them that I went back and collected all the Red Cross wool, because nobody wore it anyhow—mufflers, gloves, socks, sweaters and hats. I had two bags of this, and a corporal helped me. I was a buck private, the youngest and the lowest of the whole army, and he helped me. And then I raided our commissariat tent, and I took every damn thing. I filled a whole sack. We carried the food in a sack and the two bags of wool, and we gave it all to the Belgians, to these poor people because they could pull this wool and make something out of it. They were wonderful with needles. And I figured that out. I was a kid figuring all these damn things out. The corporal said, 'They're going to raise hell with us for stealing the food.'"

"I said, 'I wouldn't care, what the hell....' You don't care after a while."

"And then came Christmas. I think we were relieved from the front. We were there, and we were lined up, and the French sent a band with these big horns and trumpets and things playing that "Radetsky March"—no, the Hungarians play the "Radetsky March." "The French March.""

"Then, lo and behold, I see some of the Belgian men, coming down the road...dressed nicely, as much as they could, cleaned up. And they came and went right up to the Captain and thanked him for his goodness for sending all the wool and the food. And he hit the ceiling. 'Now I know where the food went! Who the hell did it?'"

Did they catch up with you?
"Oh, sure. He was going to go nuts. So I stepped out and said, 'I did it.' He raised hell. 'Now I know where the food went.' Then after it was all over, nothing happened, just yelling. Nothing ever happened to me."

"I left the army after the armistice [*November 11, 1918*] for thirty-some days and went to Paris. Everybody did. The whole of Paris was full of officers, up to majors, from the second division. They just walked out…. Hell, the war was over. And I was there. I was always lucky, lucky as hell. I don't know if it was brains or just fool's luck or stupid luck. The corporal was half Indian, from Oklahoma. He was a wild bastard, and I could trust him. He was about the only one I could trust. He was in the regular army, and he was supposed to know better than everybody else. But he didn't give a damn about the war."

"We all went to Paris, and they knew I was a virgin. I had never slept with a woman. The whole damned army knew. And the major called me in. This was when we were going on proper leave. We were supposed to go to Grenoble. We were in the army eleven months without a pass. And then you began to fight with everybody. Everybody was crazy. And the doctor called me in, and said, 'You're the only one that doesn't go out with women, but here's a whole kit that you have to take care of. And give these people medical care on leave.'"

"And we got out. And everyone…the first thing my corporal did was get a girl, and they went out rowing and she stole his watch. That I'll never forget. He was going to go out and kill her. I said, 'You will if you don't stop it.' He had a knife. He was going to go out and cut her head off—he was so wild. He got his watch back. I think he frightened the daylights out of her."

"So he would have left about fifteen men who were not cured yet. We had a wonderful doctor, a major who was really a realist about how to get over this thing. And here these men were in the war—or the whole damn company—and they were going be left behind…. It's a hell of a situation—you're just not even a replacement, and you're just nothing so far as the army is concerned. So he said, 'There's one way that they can't inspect you.' You see, you had to be inspected by a series of doctors—'and that is if I circumcise you. Then you'll be put in splints, and we'll time it and use bandages and everything, and we'll say that you were converted or some damn thing.' Well, everybody knew about it so most of them said, 'Okay.' They were circumcised and put in splints, and we got to Bordeaux and were inspected, and everybody came home. You had to time it. He was right there and he said, 'No, these people have converted to Judaism; they had to be circumcised.'

"But I had this kit, and I told everybody, 'You have to come to me, I'm in charge of this damn thing.' And I gave them all this medicine for venereal disease. And the curious thing was all the stations. That's what the major didn't want. He was the one who circumcised the men. He said, 'Don't go near the prophylactic stations, because they're all police stations.' So if you'd stayed over, and your pass wasn't still any good, you'd have been arrested. And you know what color the stations were? They were green. All of the prophylactic stations were green, like our police stations here. But the military police were in there, too. What a wacky army."

"The major said, 'I can trust you in everything.' And I said, 'Okay.' But they made me a first class private when I came back. That was a scandal—how the hell could the youngest man in the regiment be a first class private? We're stupid, but he must be stupider. Then they'd come to me. In a curious way people always have come to me, even as a boy, they'd come for advice, or this or that thing. I'd figure out how they could do this and that and the other thing. And, boy, if the army ever heard me giving advice to soldiers: 'If you want to go, just get on the train and go.' You didn't pay for any tickets."

"One fellow went to southern France and then to Spain and he came back, and he became an MP. I said, 'How the hell can you become an MP?' 'Well,' he said, 'Go down to Spain. They may be nice down there.' The next thing I knew he had deserted and gone to Spain."

"Christ, what a life. Even on the transport going over…All the lights were out. We had two thousand white soldiers and two thousand Negro soldiers. The Negro soldiers were labor battalions from the South. You could see whales shooting spouts. And these men would gather on the black purple (that was the only light you could use on the passage) with bibles. You couldn't see a goddamned thing, but they couldn't read either. And they were more frightened of whales, on account of the story of Jonah and the whale, than they were of submarines. They didn't know about submarines, but they were frightened of whales."

"So one day, one of the black men said, 'Would you tell me how we can sleep? Because we're so packed in down there.' And I said, 'Why don't you come on deck and sleep on deck?' because it was nice, soft weather. 'Oh, no—the whales.'

That's when I heard about the whales. The whales were liable to swallow them."

"We were shot at. We lost two battalions of our regiment when they sank the *Tuscany*. Then we followed. The first and the second battalion went, then the third and forth came. I was in the third battalion. The *Tuscany* was torpedoed off Ireland, and most of them were killed on the rocks there."

"And then we were shot at, at about seven or seven thirty in the morning. I saw the damn thing, the wake. It just missed us by about fifteen feet, this torpedo. We didn't give a goddamn what happened. In a sense, we were pretty tough. We were tougher than the kids going to war today because everybody worked. We were tough as hell, and had boxing matches on the deck, and all kinds of activity that you could laugh at. I laughed all during the war, you know—and it was tragic up front. But then came the end of the war, and I decided to leave. I said, 'Jesus, I'm going to go.' So I jumped on the train and went to Paris. And the corporal was with me. We wandered around; we had a couple of dollars. I sent word to my brother so he sent me a couple of dollars. And I said, 'I may come down and visit you.' He was a naval aviator, outside of Bordeaux."

"We stayed two weeks in Paris and got away with murder. I only talked to MPs (marines were MPs) not the army. I had no pass or anything. We were sleeping all over, in the YMCA and every damn thing. You always find a place. But you're liable to get picked up any minute. And you're in a hell of a fix if you do. They were picking up officers, up to majors in rank. So I said, 'I'm going to the military police headquarters' [*at Saint*

Anne Hotel]. The corporal wouldn't come up. He said, 'They'll just throw you in the jug. You have no pass of any kind.'"

"I said, 'Come up with me.' Oh, no, he wouldn't come. So he stayed outside, or he sat in the lobby and looked at something as if he was wise. He didn't have a pass, either; he could have been picked up. So I was in the line. I had white hair…You know I had blond white hair. And I was called 'Whitey' or 'White Mountain.' I was called every damn thing. I had to live these things down. Well, the curious thing was, that while standing in line with all kinds of officers, of all kinds of ranks—sergeants, corporals, everything, buck privates—I saw a sergeant of the Marine Corps, sitting at the desk, and a lieutenant, and he and I had graduated from school in the same class. He was named McGonagle, a crazy Irishman. His father owned a saloon. That's the only thing I remember. He was in the Marine Corps and got himself wounded at Chateau Thierry. And I said, 'How the hell did you become a sergeant?'"

"'Oh,' he said, 'I got wounded and everything like that. And they thought I was going to die and whatever.' He was badly wounded, so they made him a desk sergeant. He said, 'Get the hell over here.' He pulled me out of the line and I sat in back of him so the lieutenant couldn't see me, and he wrote out my pass and he handed it to the lieutenant. All the lieutenant was doing was stamping them, just stamping the pass and never questioning anything. And so I was made an MP, if you want to know."

"I lived in that goddamned Saint Anne hotel as a guest, with a badge and a pistol, and I could go anyplace. McGonagle and I went out on the town. We went to everything for free because we were MPs. He said, 'For Christ's sake, don't get caught with these. I can keep the lieutenant, he's drunk all the time, I can keep him quiet.' I lived right with the marines. So I got the corporal, and said, 'I have a friend.' He said, 'Bring him up.' So we went all over Paris alone. My friend and I traveled together. We were the same age—my God, just kids. We went to the Folies Bergères and The Moulin Rouge. Everything was free; we just walked in."

"We never dreamed of stopping a person. I said, 'For Christ sakes, you're not going to pull anything when I'm with you! Don't dare stop anybody.' He didn't. He said, 'This is only for protection—so that we won't get picked up. For Christ sakes, don't get picked up.' So he had to get me a hat. I had a soldier hat."

"I stayed there a couple of weeks, and he said, 'I'm being transferred home, and I have to be operated on there, but I'll get you on the train.' I didn't want to march into Germany. Fifteen days with a hundred pounds, ninety pounds or something, plus all your souvenirs … You carried every damn thing. Oh, it weighed like hell. I got to Metz, then I got to Nancy, then I was at the Gare du Nord. I'll never forget that thing. He got me in. We went in the train with our badges, you know, and got in the first class toilet and locked the door because they'll search the train."

"And I got in there, and there were two American officers, a captain and a lieutenant, from the second division, and two French officers plus the two of us. We were all sitting on the toilet, on the basin, bullshitting away. AWOL. Everybody going up to the line. The war was over. They were marching into Germany—our place was around Coblenz—and I didn't want that goddamned march."

"'I got through,' McGonagle said. 'As soon as the train gets out in the country, throw everything, the badge and pistol, out of the window. Don't get caught with it.' I told the captain how I was made an MP, and they didn't believe the goddamned story. I said, 'You have to believe it, here's my badge and pistol.' And I heaved the forty-five out, because if you got caught with it, it was holy hell."

So I got up there, and I was only arrested once on that expedition—by my own company MP at the railroad station. He said, 'They're looking all over hell for you. They think you deserted.' I said, 'I went to Paris.' I was called up and court martialed, but nothing happened. They just raised hell. They have to because I dared and took chances. I was innocent in many things, but nobody would have done the crazy things I did."

"How long ago was 1918? I was wounded just fifty-two years ago today, January fourth, nineteen eighteen. This is the day I'll never forget. You see what an impression that made on me? January fourth, no matter what happens, that's my day."

6 | *ABOUT SOUND*

"I think you have to hear tones as no one else hears them."

"But to hear that sound—there's a definite sound there…and until you hear, you don't know if you're coming or going or if what you're trying to do is coming or going. It's all mixed up and it's all scattered. There won't be any sense until you hear that sound. If you can hear that sound, no matter what happens it'll be right. Otherwise you're figuring out all the bad things, good things, but that sound is the whole picture. That's the whole expression. And that's the way I'm placing my life. I want to hear that sound and I'm making every effort under the sun. It is not like hearing a bell or anything, but I want to hear that whole place, that ice house, ring as it could—the only place on the whole plantation that could ring, like the Aeolian harp—if there's enough usage and tone coming out of everything, every person and every thing. If it's *used*, suddenly you'll hear the sound of that piece. And it will be a sound, an understanding, a possibility that could come out of that kind of thing."

"I had it out with Mme. de Salzmann last summer. I went down and we sat talking. She's very much interested in what I'm doing with these tones and sounds and expression and that where there's movement there has to be a sound. And I said, 'In everything…it doesn't have to be the Movements, but in the movement of the people you're close to and working with, if the Movements were taught—not that they had to be doing it perfectly, but to create an atmosphere of contact with their neighbors all around—to try to make contact with their people instead of attempting to do the Movements correctly and everybody is out of their existence, then there is a definite sound. If a whole group can make contact, there's a definite sound.'"

She said, 'I know exactly what you mean. We started to do the Movements to this picture, and then I stopped after a week, and I said we're not getting any place, we're not doing anything, and I think we won't do it any more. And then they said, 'Let's have a meeting,' and they sat up all night and talked it all over. The next day, they came in and they were electrified—they hadn't slept. And I heard the sound. There was a definite sound.' And she said, 'Then I knew that we could go ahead and make the film.' I said, 'Then you know what I'm attempting.' And she said, 'Oh, absolutely.'"

"'What have you got to express?' That's what Casals said in every lesson. (I saw him on the television). 'Try to put something of your own into it. Don't just read the notes, but put something of you into the expression.'"

"And that's what I always tell you about Paderewski. He made mistakes on purpose. The Lanier family over in Greenwich had a pianola, and someone who read the whole score as it was playing said, 'I counted five mistakes.' This was reported to Paderewski, and he said, 'You have to put something of yourself into the record. It wouldn't be right to play a perfect piece.' You understand? I think that is the great lesson: What is your expression?"

"It can't just be read as notes, or whatever; that's why I'm fooling around with tone. I think you have to hear tones as no one else hears them. Not crazy. I mean you can hear various things no matter how deaf you are. You have to see, also. But for people to come with scientific data on tone…that is the least I'm interested in. I don't want to get involved with that. I don't even want to think about it because I don't want to look for that. I want to have access to that, but I don't want to look for it. A Zen piece on tone was one of the best things I've read—the different signals with tone; they all know the pitch of the different bells, the timbre of everything that is being banged. Well, that is something. Then, of course, the great thing that can happen in the course of time…as the saying was years ago: 'Try to hear your own echo.' Not your own voice but your own *echo*."

When did you first get interested in sound?
"All my life. You see, I could sing. I sang all the time. That was the thing. When I was a boy, I sang, for my existence. Thank God Carnegie Hall existed. Carnegie Hall was my musical education. After a while it didn't matter what they played—that was the thing. And when I heard my first cho-

rus, I thought it was out of this world. It was something about St. Francis. Who wrote it, or what it was, I don't know, but it was wonderful for me."

"Then, when I heard Bach's music with horns for the first time…. I heard it again in Notre Dame cathedral. We were listening to the B Minor Mass, and during the intermission they did Bach with horns, long horns, all sizes, in the choir loft over the entrance. It was out of this world. And it is made for a big space like Notre Dame. There were about 6,500 people all jammed in, and once you got in you never got out, not even for intermission. They played this from behind you. You wouldn't think you'd be interested in anything so loud and blaring, but it was beautiful. The whole B Minor Mass was sung by the choir from St. Eustache."

"Music is civilized civilization. I went through this whole thing because I didn't know any better. That was the thing to do, so I heard every kind of artist and music, every kind of sound, until I graduated from that. And you wouldn't think you'd graduate. I have graduated."

"There are people who go crazy because they hear sounds. Maybe people think you're crazy if you hear sounds. But you don't hear sounds psychologically—you actually hear things."

"That's one of my curious idiosyncrasies: how movement without sound affects me. Ballet affected me, and I never knew why, until I'm coming closer to why."

If ballet, or a great movement of humans was done objectively—as we're attempting to do in the Movements, as objectively as possible—perhaps I would have heard a sound. But seeing as how there wasn't any sound, I used to become ill, physically ill—all this movement and nothing. It was just movement. And there has to be movement, but the sound has to be there, too, and I could never understand why I was affected."

"You know, we go through the horror of our accidental birth and existence, because everyone is born by accident. There's no doubt of that; there's hardly any person born by design. But here we are, believing—believing in our little miracle thing—that this is the right thing for us, that this is the truth. Many discouragements come. Many things happen in the course of a lifetime, but this is our belief, without looking toward a larger sphere of existence that encompasses this whole universe, because you could be part of that. Not to make judgment, but here it is. And it is not to say I accept this way, but here it is. And in a curious way, while you're living tissue, do something about that existence. Just do something about that existence while you're alive."

"You know, the greatest miracle I can find in my depth is that we can see. We're able to see and observe. How in the hell does that happen? Of course all the senses are a miracle, and of course, I'm working on sound now. What is sound? But to be able to see is a very strange thing. I don't know if you ever thought of such things."

"The five senses exist; but according to the Old Man there were seven senses and we've lost two. H.G. Wells wrote about another world where people were blind but they had developed another sense. I feel very deeply that was the sense of perception most of mankind had at one time, and now it's lost."

"Now, there are people who are born with a strong sense of perception, greater than other people. It's not that these people are better, but they happened to be born with a greater sense of perception. These people are not great, and that's the curious thing—the normality of them, even with greater insight, with greater keenness. It's not that these people are greater than others, just normal. God knows what the other senses were, but I suspect that perception was one of them."

"If a man forgets, he dies, or he is lost. 'Dies' is a pretty strong word for that. If he forgets, he's lost, until he remembers again. But that fits what we're talking about, which is the effect of sound.

"As Mr. Gurdjieff used to say, 'I'll smell that tone.' He talked like that. And then he'd give us a lecture on how each note in the scale produced a whole scale within itself. If you're sensitive to that, you can hear parts of that scale. These are probably some of the overtones we hear in the Aeolian harp. We hear two different things. But it follows so much, say, *one*: the overcoming one is true; and the echo—not the echo—the loudest one, is something else again. And that off thing, with another cymbal or bell, could straighten itself out and, probably from the two of them could make the most beautiful sound."

"It's like the Greek cathedrals being built off-plumb. The columns are just off on purpose. From a distance they look absolutely perfect, and the effect is due to this, their being off.

That's what I mean by that off-sound which, with another sound as a part of a whole group of sounds, will become perfect to our ear. But it wasn't just the one sound — there are two of them. I felt with my fingers, the two of them are different. That's why I said to John Lust about the cast Tibetan bells, 'You have to keep them numbered, one and two all the time. If you make two out of one, you won't get the effect.'"

"We'll see. It's a big story. It's a big undertaking. But I can see some of the great possibilities if I follow, think of, and remember the principle. The idea has to be remembered, but the principle has to be adhered to. If we follow that principle, I bet you we could come to something, that no one would know how the hell we found it."

"Now in this Yale singing tower, or the Harkness Tower, or that cathedral in Italy where you can sing with your echo — that kind of construction — if it was done objectively, just imagine."

"You can see where we're losing out on that score in the music hall in Lincoln Center. They got all kind of scientists, and engineers with their airplane wings, and still it doesn't sound right because they've lost the art of construction. They begin with just four straight walls and a ceiling and then try to make it effective enough where you can hear all over, and still it's not constructed right. It doesn't reverberate, it doesn't *sound*. Maybe it does now, but it didn't for years. Carnegie Hall is the most perfect hall I've heard, I think on account of the thickness of its walls — they're about six feet thick. That's how I became interested in sound. All my life I've been interested in sound. I got into music, but I didn't get deeply into it. I can't read a damn note—but I can hear and know."

"I more or less recognize what's playing. I could recognize everything years ago. I heard more than most people, and I saw more than most people. I think that, in your education—not formal education, but education of your senses, by repeated usage and usage and usage, like that theory of the violin and the Aeolian harp—there may be sounds like where a heavy cloud has to go over greenery or water to pull it out."

"There's a theory that I've heard, also about wind. No one knows if the wind is pushed or it's pulled, and if so how we hear it. No one knows. It's proved by the practice in California and Arizona of seeding the clouds. The rain doesn't fall there at all, because there isn't anything there to attract it and to pull it out until the clouds hit land as they go east, where they don't need the water. So you can put that theory into sound."

Did you talk to Mr. Gurdjieff about sound?
"No, we had talks about sounds and music, but nothing in great detail as I am going into it now. When speaking about sound, you have to remember there are places on the earth where people live in perfect valleys like that one in the Cape Verde islands where they whistle, and the sound hits the walls in order to travel down the valley, and everybody understands every whistle. It's like being in prison and hearing the various codes and signals. There are sympathetic things. And this

has to be with all the senses. When they have accumulated enough, with all the senses more or less in harmony and as objectively as possible, this is the type of thing that could effect people when you introduce the force of the five senses that we have, and maybe a sixth or a seventh sense with it, such as perception ... and there may be other senses that we just tap and touch upon and not know it."

"A couple of years ago, Peggy Flinsch's young daughter, when she was a tiny little girl, looked at me when we walked in and started yelling and pointing, and she ran to her mother, and she never took her eyes off me, and then she started to talk. It was a curious thing, a whole chemical thing that she was shaken by. It was, as one would say, 'love at first sight,' and this child was affected as soon as she saw me. But she had to be in a certain position in order to be affected. We had never seen one another before. She sat with me all the time, because she knew she was affected—that's the curious thing. And no one could make any head or tail of it. I said, 'This is chemistry.'"

"You see, it isn't only the senses. Something else has to be introduced. It can't only be the senses; it has to be a greater force, but you would never come to that greater force without the enhancing of the senses. This is a great theory of mine."

"I read about things here and there. That little Indian book helps me a great deal because it tells of definite movements and uses of the senses, but there's a greater force. You don't graduate. And that helps you to arrive and recognize your greater force. And that's where I think I can get some kind of understanding, because suddenly there will be a whole rush of ideas and thoughts, an understanding to make what I was talking about feasible, to make it possible—suddenly all kinds of things could be added to make the most strange effect. There's no reason they can't affect one another. But I want to project differently, even affect a group of bells over here that would affect that again."

"When I was in France, a woman said, 'Well, with the sound of things... the passage in *Beelzebub*... cosmic harmony, celestial sound... have you ever tried to make such a thing?'"

"I said, 'No!' Everybody roared when I said that, because whatever Mr. Gurdjieff experimented with or heard or saw I will never touch. I have not heard, and I have not experimented. I'm not trying to recreate what he talked about. That's his expression; it's not mine. I hate the idea of copying that, but if I make a design in my mind, I want to make this larger thing for casting bells, with buttresses on it, to see if we can possibly pour it. We should be able to do it: enough vents, and pour it in one mass. For some reason or other it should give a different tone."

7 | N O G E N T – L E – R O U T R O U

*"Oh, I did every damn thing under the sun. And all those places
…They added something, some kind of thing. I was working
at figuring it out—figuring out my existence."*

"I WENT TO DURHAM, to the University of New Hampshire,
but I quit because I was furious with them. I said, 'You're not
teaching me farming. I want to learn something here.' Then I
went to France."

"That's just when they begin plowing—January. You
know, it's in the Beauce country. I plowed with four white
oxen. They were Italian, snow white with big horns. I learned
how to strap them up and walk them into the pen. We had a
drinking pen; they walk into the water and drink. They were
terribly tame and very well trained."

"We had this curious plow. It was two plows and you stay
on this furrow and plow out. One team walks in the trench
and the other walks on the top. You came to the end, turned
them around, and reversed the plow—flip it over and this
other plow would take the furrow instead of going around
and around. I plowed the whole damn day. And then we

would stop and get something to eat or whatever, a big chunk of bread and some cheese and some pickled herring that you had to heat over a fireplace on a long iron fork every morning. I'd make myself sandwiches of that, and then I had this cider—I carried a keg, a small hand-made keg of hard cider. Just slung it over my shoulder. We ate five big meals a day but this was collation. And I would eat this and drink this cider. Oh, I had a hell of a good life, with the animals and doing what I pleased. We had collation twice a day. You had to eat, because we worked fourteen to sixteen hours a day. And that was something."

"First thing you did in the morning was get up and run like hell over the cobblestones to feed the horses. You had to pour stuff into a trough and spread it out so they wouldn't gulp it down. These were the special horses. They were worth ten or fifteen thousand dollars. They were priceless anyhow—the prize animals of France, all stallions. Then we'd come back and eat breakfast, and eat a hell of a breakfast. It lasted for hours. All kinds of food. That's the place they had the cheese that had to walk. If it didn't walk it was no good. Oh, my God, what discussions. And everyone had a knife and was slicing the bread, talking at the same time, and all the bull that went on. And then the patron would come in and lay the law down."

"You know, we had hundreds of animals in that damn place. I guess there must have been ten men, just taking care of the horses. 'Course, I was just an outsider...And then he hired about forty or forty-five Poles who'd migrate each year for the harvest. They did the wheat, the bundling of the wheat; and the potatoes, dug all the potatoes. Everything was gathered—and then, suddenly, two big stills arrived in the courtyard, big gigantic things, and you make as much Calvados as you possibly can in two weeks. We had barrels as big as this room, made in the basement, never moved, but they distilled raw cider into Calvados; it must have been a hundred and fifty proof. It was the wildest drink I ever had in my life."

"Well, we did everything there, and they fired this by wood, boiling, stewing all the time. Excitement all the time going on."

"Then in the fall came the pig killer and he looked exactly like a pig. He was a funny little runty creature. And they had big pigs—they save them for two years; we kill ours in a year … in less than a year. They had the cellar door open, and the pig killer would get hammering down steel spikes into the ground, and he'd get the pig on there and tie him down and stick him, with all the women in the kitchen, four or five of them, waiting with long-handled iron frying pans to collect the blood, and then run into the fireplace and curdle the blood to make blood wurst out of it. I never saw such excitement in all my life."

"And then the women helped him. He cut the pig into square chunks, never saving any part of the pig, hams or anything, and it was put in big crocks, in brine, salted right then with heavy rock salt and put in the basement. When that came to be eaten, that stuff, it was boiled. The salt had gone through it, and it came out just like a piece of lard. Just as white as snow and I said, 'Jeez, I wouldn't eat that for anything.' And they would get a chunk and take a slice and put it on the bread. Oh, my God, I died just looking at the thing. So one time they said, "Just put pepper on it", and I did, and it was just wonderful. And then I used to make sandwiches of it, but I couldn't take the whiteness."

"There was fresh cream all the time, and fresh butter, and fresh milk. The women did everything. They worked like hell. The French work like the devil. We had a brick floor, and every day that brick floor was scrubbed. And we ate the best food I've ever eaten in my life: roasts, turkeys, ducks, pigeon pie and whatever came off the land. Sunday was the deadly day. They bought a big chunk of beef, beautiful, and then they boiled it. That was the Sunday lunch—until everybody escaped it. I escaped it after a while. It was wonderful, but who the hell wanted it?"

"So the son and I had a car, a little tiny car. It was like a bathtub. He sat in the front, and I sat in the back. And we went all over. 'Let's go to a horse race.' Well, La Ferté Bernard was the horse race. And somebody came along and we had a race. The gas tank was outside, and was to test how far a liter would go. So a man came along and said, 'What is that?' And so Robert... he said, 'Oh, that's to catch flies.' And we were both arrested. It was the mayor. The two of us got put in jail. And we had to call up Avaline to come and get us—he has that power. That's a life! And three or four times we got into grave difficulties."

"That was Sunday. We went to the horse race and bet five francs on the race. And the spectators came out in costumes.

I don't know if you've ever been in the country where they come out in costumes of 1860...and the women...and the men in a funny little hat...wild! And then they go to a restaurant and the man never takes his hat off at all."

"Where the hell else were we arrested? I was arrested in Le Mans. I was going to a horse show and we had to load the horses on the railroad cars. We had an Englishman with us whose father owned the Pomeroy Champagne, and he had fits. He was an insipid creature. And he was leading two stallions—he was between them. I was in back of him and I was watching him. I had two pretty wild animals there. And he had a fit, right under the two horses, and they sensed this right away, and I had all I could do to call one of the men to grab my horses, and I got him out of there...to keep him from getting killed. I sat him on the curb and took charge of the horses; and one horse they led up into the gangway, and the other one got wild. We were loading at a railroad loading station, and the horse ran around and dragged me right through the railroad station out across the goddamn tracks, and here I was—under him and over him and every place, just hanging on for dear life, with everyone watching us like a circus act. Right through the railroad station and never stopped...And I'm hanging on. Well, we finally got him onto the train."

"It was a long trip to Le Mans. The train was full of horses and the French government pays for it, but if anything happens you get no insurance. Can't collect a thing, and we had our prize animals on there...So, a peasant from another crew went to sleep with a cigarette, and the train caught on fire. It caught on fire about a mile before we hit the great trestle that goes into Le Mans. There's no walking space on this trestle. The train was on fire and the horses were kicking the sides out of the railroad cars and going overboard, with flames going for about ten cars. I saw it and yelled to the men to tell the engineer to quickly get off the trestle, and we'd drain the water out of the engine. We did, and we formed a line overhead, and got the fire out and uncoupled the cars, but one of our two-year-olds, a prize animal, got badly burned."

"That was the time I got arrested, I think. The French were bastards; they blamed everybody but the engineer. But he was no good—he just kept moving the train slowly. He had to stop or else go on and we'd get on land. Well, I raised hell because I knew exactly what to do. We uncoupled the cars which weren't burning and then had him pull up, and we put out the fire, but our horses died right and left. Prize animals of France. And I raised so much hell that they put me in jail. I didn't give a damn. The French can put you in jail for nothing. If you raise enough hell they'll blame you for the fire or some damn thing. That used to worry me about France."

"What a lousy thing that was! Avaline came and got me out. Then I sat up all night and we put ice bags on the horse. He stood in ice bags with a bellyband under him. He was burned and he had to perform the next day. And we had to get that fever down. You know, when you get burned you get fever. We gave him shots. But then they bleed horses in France, and Avaline took a bucket and a half of blood. A little plunger that fits in a tube, and you hit the plunger and it goes right in, and the blood just pours out in a stream. And he was expert at it. That's to relieve the pressure on the head and whatever. They're not allowed to do that here. We got the horse in shape, and we showed him, and we won first prize. He was the most beautiful animal and very calm, and he made his paces and did all his routine, stood still, etc. He was really a prize animal. I have pictures somewhere."

"I used to ride and exercise the horses, including a big white horse called Caduc. He was the four year old. And he was the one who won all the prizes. He was first rate. I used to ride him a great deal."

"Another time I was leading ten horses eleven kilometers from the other farm, and in every little town, or hamlet, I bought tangerines and ate tangerines all the way over."

"There's a curious thing I learned in the courtyard. You line the horses up and there's a halter, and the halter is woven into the tail of the horse behind until his head is held tightly, and by pulling his tail he can't kick that horse. They're all pretty wild. And then you get them running in a circle to tire them out, in a long line, and then you get an older horse leading, and he's the one you control with a forked stick. Sometimes, if they're wild, they'll pile on one another and get all tangled up. And we were moving I guess about a hundred horses, in groups of ten, strung out for miles. When I came to Nogent we had to go through the whole town. By that time they were worn out, and didn't want to fight any more."

"I didn't have any more trouble until I came to the *octroi*. They put down a bar and you have to pay a tax for each horse. I hated like hell to stop because then the horses get into a … So he put the bar down, in a vicious way …. I almost told him to go to hell, except I couldn't go through. I said, 'You call up Mr. Avaline and he'll pay,' and I explained as well as I could. 'Oh,' he said, 'I can't do this.' He knew I was a foreigner. Then somebody else walked up and told him to go to hell, and we walked through. He wanted to collect a tax for each horse and myself, but the men told him don't bother with me. But that's a law, this tax business. He could have called the police there. But we got through the town very well and got in, and all was well, and they were put in the field. It was a marvelous experience, I tell you."

"About a mile away was a crossroads, and as I was crossing, a car came and tooted with his little horn, and the horse (you're never afraid of him because … you're just not afraid of him) but he kicked me and jumped on me. I was under him and all around him. Then I went plunging into the damn wall, and he went on. He went home, and they all went out to see where the hell I was. I was knocked cold. I thought I was broken up, but I wasn't. I told them what happened. They said, 'He was born on a horse' and still I was thrown and broke a leg."

"Another time another man broke an arm. There were things like that happening every damn day. It wasn't anything if I got messed up, but you never leave your horse. You hang onto him for dear life. There's nothing to it; you just don't become frightened, that's all. The worst is one who gets blind and backs up. He'll back into anything and there's nothing you can do. The only thing you can do is what the French do. When I was at the Prieuré, they had riding horses next door, and one had backed right into our corner. The help came out and put a bag over his head, and the man bent his tail and cut his tail until the blood shot out, way out. Then they led him in, and that's the last I ever heard of him. You never see things like that happen here—they're not allowed to happen—but the French know horses more than we do."

It was to study horses and horse breeding that you went to Avaline, wasn't it?
"Yes. And this was the best place I've ever seen. I never saw castration and bleeding. The government inspects all horses twice a year in the square. And they'll tell you if that horse can breed or not breed and, if not, he has to be castrated. He wasn't allowed to ruin the breed. And he didn't look bad at all, this horse. I don't know what the hell was against him. I think they just do it once a year. Pick out a horse! Avaline knew horses—boy! He knew horses. I never saw a man concentrate so much. He knew exactly what to do. He was a great salesman."

"He'd do any goddamn thing, and he had the best horses in France. We had two thousand hectares (and you know a hectare is about two and a quarter acres) and six or seven hundred stallions on the prairie at one time. It was worth your life to go out among them. They'd charge you, bite you, and kick you. That's how I learned to ride. Get close to one and grab his mane and throw your leg over. And go galloping like mad across the prairie. Clamp your legs tight. That's the way you break him in. Run him like mad—not in a small place but in a big area, and he'd run for miles, and then he'd be too tired to run back, and then you're all right. He'd slowly get used to you. You control the spinal column, and they don't kick—use a forked wood stick. And then I had one…He was placid, sort of. My head just came to the top of his back, a stallion, a Percheron. I was standing, scrubbing him, and he just moved his foot. He stepped right on my foot and stood there. So what do you do? You can't give him a shove because he weighs over a ton."

"Oh, I did every damn thing under the sun. And all those places…They added something, some kind of thing. I was working at figuring it out—figuring out my existence. It was good. Because I did it, and now that's over. I have no more desire of doing that sort of thing. I learned a hell of a lot. That's why I couldn't take the pomposity of some of the English at Mendham. I knew they weren't going anywhere. I still can't take them, so what the hell."

"We had a horse show once under the Eiffel tower. The Eiffel tower covers four acres—it's tremendous. They just put up canvas all around the legs, made a circus tent out of it. We had a big horse show there. It was wonderful. The French are very good about a thing like that. Just imagine us using some big area for a horse show without an army of police protection. It's putrid. The whole damn thing is crazy."

"Maurice was a man, about thirty-five, who looked fifty-five. Hard-working peasant type, knew horses and was always angry. And I think Maurice was envious of Voisin; he was the boss—more or less the working boss. He was terribly nice, and he was from Brittany, and he had two red cheeks. I tell you he looked like the 'chauve souris,' the ballet, with red cheeks, painted on. Maurice met a woman who was much older, probably thirty years older, who had money, and she had a farm. She must have been a high class, more or less successful peasant. And she fell in love with Maurice, and he came back and told us all about it. He said, 'I'm going to marry her.' Because he wanted the farm Maurice finally married her, and he came back on a Sunday and said how wrong everything was. I asked him, 'Are you going to stick it out or what the hell?' He said, 'Well, I have the farm now, and that's what I wanted.' And he stuck with her until he owned the whole goddamned place. She died and left him everything, and most likely that's what he wanted."

"Well, it was the wildest damned romance you ever heard in your life: Maurice with this woman who came out in a costume that must have been handed down for generations. About an 1876 female costume on St. Jean's day. That I'll never forget as long as I live. I met her then. That's a holy day, the one day for all the peasants, all the servants. That's the official day that you change your job if you want to change your job. Everybody meets in the town square. It's a fête day—the greatest fête day I've ever seen. Peasants come out in costumes that are out of this world, all decked out in funny straw hats. All probably knowing a patron they would love to work for. Everybody is there, including our patron, Louis Avaline. And I was with his son, Robert. And he just wanted to raise hell."

"That's the time I couldn't find where the *pissoir* was. The goddamn mayor had moved the *pissoir* in front of the hotel because he couldn't get graft out of the hotel. The town *pissoir* was on that wall, way over there—open, a big trough. He had it moved directly in front of the hotel. I said, 'What the hell happened?' I was fascinated. Avaline said, 'Well, the new mayor from Paris was a bastard. He wanted the graft from the hotel and they refused to pay because they didn't know him.' And so he had the *pissoir* moved. Wasn't that something? Christ, I loved that."

"Then we had to go across the square and come to the ancient arch. That was the north gate. It had a big arch you had to go under, very narrow, just for a cart. Then on a hill there was a Roman fortress, square, an absolute square stone fortress on the mountainside. And outside the walls, on the whole hillside, were all the peasants who had no farms or anything; they were squatters. They had squatters' rights like in ancient Roman times. And suddenly I heard the news from Avaline that a new premier of France had been elected, who was born in Nogent-le-Routrou. And Avaline said, 'My God, what's going to happen to us? He's crazy. Everybody knows him—he's insane!' About 1924 or '25 they had the Paris world's fair, and I saw that. Now, this man wanted to see the fair at night. He was the premier! Wearing his nightshirt, he hung out of the car to see what they were passing. He leaned out of the car, and they struck a tunnel. And he was dragged out of the car in his nightshirt. He was dead, of course. That was the end of the premier of France. And Avaline came and said, 'I told you he was crazy.'"

"That's the way the French are. I knew he was crazy. Can you imagine anybody leaning out of a car at night? He must have been off his rocker. But that happened anyhow, in our town. My God, between the *octroi*, the premier, and the *pissoir*—and my lady friends who lived in the opposite direction—I had a hell of a good time in that town. This town was something. The war went through it. You can imagine what the hell happened there."

How long were you there, all told?
"Oh, I was there a couple of years. I had to get a permit after two weeks in France...they're so strict about it. The college professor whom I had been seeing said, 'You have to have a permit to stay.' So I said, 'Well, the hell with it.' 'No,' he said, 'you have to get one of these permits.' So he said, 'But then you have to have someone go with you.' Well, I knew no Frenchmen there, so in two weeks I was sent out to Nogent-le-Routrou, and I forgot all about the damn permit to stay. So Avaline came to me and said, 'My God, have you got a permit to stay because everybody in the whole damn town knows you're here?' The grapevine, the gossip and everything—you know what the rumor was? That I had escaped from prison in the US and ran for France. Avaline said, 'They're all talking about you.' I was so blond, and going around as if nothing in the world affected me. He said, 'They think you escaped from prison.' So then he came to me and said, 'Have you got your permit to stay? Because, my God, if you don't....' So he went with me to the local *Mairie* and wrote it all out, and

then every so many months I'd have to report. But it wasn't a working permit. Oh, I enjoyed all these rumors. It's like a small village here. If a stranger walks the street in the pitch dark, they'd know there was a stranger in town. So they knew I was in town for no reason at all except that I was new."

"A hell of a lot of fun. I enjoyed my life there. In a curious way, I had a hell of a good time. It was serious. I worked like mad all the time, and serious. And I really went places with myself. I moved over to another village—Verrière was the name of the village, but that was the name of the property. He had a hell of a big ranch there also, so he said, 'Do you want to go over there and look that place over?' And I said, 'Okay,' and I went over there. That's where he had a lot of that very rich milk, milk so rich it tasted like evaporated milk. We made all the cheese, all the butter, sweet butter, every damn thing on the property, killed the pigs, made blood wurst, and oh, Christ, I really lived like a king there."

8 | SPEAKING IN GROUPS

*"The awfulness of the world may be the
greatest thing that's happened to this world."*

"THE REASON I'M IN THIS KIND OF WORK IS, and I feel quite sure
in saying this, that this has more force than I do. Therefore
I will be part of it in order to help me gain more force. That
may not seem to make sense, but it does. Once you have accepted this work, you have taken a part of a force that actually does not belong to you. As simply as I can say this, you
have taken a part of God's force, because this is His job, if
you want to know—to pull people together. You have taken
a part of this force upon yourself, to do it yourself. And forever and ever and ever, you are both blessed and cursed. You
cannot blame anyone but yourself. And you know of nothing
better, because you have struck a core of something that exists, and therefore you work toward that core. So, someone
say something so that we can be more or less together."

"The extreme effect that I can think of is where I get a real
shiver right through me, when I look at that, when that hap-

pens to me now, I say that's something that I have absorbed and will never, never forget; it's part of my existence now."

"The other thing is a quandary; the big mystery is why we're born at all, and why we live on this planet. Surely most of the people on the planet haven't been in existence as civilized people. Even the best educated did some terrible, terrible things, as they did in London, and in big cities in England, with the young blades who used to go down in the poorer sections and see what damage they could do, and then brag about it. And these were supposed to be the civilized people. We've gotten somewhat beyond that, but it does still exist. For us to attempt something greater than what is always happening is a phenomenon."

"We're trying to do something of the Absolute—which is impossible. It's up to everyone to find out where they see chaos, and ignore chaos when it comes. The man I saw on television last night, Kenneth Clark, who talks about civilization, said so many, many things that I've said here. It was the civilization of this beginning, which lasted about a hundred years, of the eighteenth and nineteenth century, and the complete slavery of these people—the women working in coal mines and things. I've seen pictures of those things, and it did exist, with a superior society who didn't see anything. And now we are existing, because this still goes on; not in these countries, but it still goes on in the world. It is a very big, deep problem that is personal for everybody—to see what they can grasp and make use of. As you often heard—I've often said this—it is civilization, or rather the attempt at civilization because they're calling a thing 'civilization' that isn't civilization, instead of our Work—not towards civilization but towards humanity. And it won't be a question of being sorry for humanity, but understanding it."

"And it's not a question of this civilization, because this is quite fouled up as it is. That is why we're attempting something impossible, with the kind of dogmatic formula that you will have to grow out of. You have to have a beginning somehow, like a child will have to start crawling, and get on chairs and go from one to the other. Somehow you have to have some kind of mechanism. And that's what we have in this interpretation, until you get to your own interpretation."

"That's about the best thing I can say to you—you work out your formula. No one has to know anything about it, but that's the way you understand it. We've read thousands of books. We've studied this, we've heard that, every word, even the comparisons of the different traditions. Things like that are all good, but you don't stick to the traditional line and stay there. That's why you said in the beginning that your Work all goes toward something that is not for your growth until you can .... I hate to use myself as an example, but I'm quite free of many things. I hope you all realize that. I go when I please. I'm a free agent."

"I wish to handle this objectively. I wish to handle these meetings, not only for my wife, but it airs my understanding of where I am. Unless there is a banter, back and forth, you don't get an answer. The awfulness of the world may be the greatest thing that's happened to this world—the opposition.

There are millions of people who want to live a good life, but there is such a terrific opposition to that."

"Russia has been an organization that's been more or less the same for a few hundred years. Instead of calling the ruler a Czar or emperor, he is the Soviet State. Their bitterness is about this country, not England, or anyplace else. It's here. Until they can bypass us in greatness, we're the enemy. They have experience with us, and there's no trust; we're the enemy, in their upbringing. It puts the people on their mettle."

"Suppose they had no enemy? It would be just like China was for hundreds or thousands of years, with people just wandering all over the place. But this opposition counts for a lot. You hate it like poison, but without the opposition, I don't think you get the shock that gives you the impetus to carry on further. I'm beginning to suspect that all systems are the same in many, many ways, except that here the emphasis is more on money than it is there. Why in the world, I always ask myself, did the Russian socialist state take over the standard, the symbol of money, instead of going into something greater?"

"Some of the suggestions you hear are pretty crazy, like wanting to make New York have larger buildings. Build big buildings…and towards what end, the enjoyment of mankind for this natural planet? There are millions and millions of people who don't believe that we're on an earthly body that's floating through space."

"I can air my views this way with you all. I have some very well thought out ideas, and there are some things I haven't thought out so well, but this idea of civilization not destroying people so much, but destroying humanity, has been with me for a long, long time. I think we'll have to outgrow this and become more humane toward everything, even the fish in the ocean. We're coming to this under great pressure; with all the pollution, we're being put on the spot by ourselves."

"I told Kenneth of a story I had seen on the television last night. It was a naturalist who made a big to-do about the mountains in British Columbia, the Cascade Range between the state of Washington and Canada. There are all kinds of wild animals living above the grass line and the tree line, just wandering around, who would be bitter enemies: panthers, bears, antelopes, badgers, and every kind of animal—young ones too, babies—and they just go and scare one another, or look at one another; but they're not killing one another off. The naturalists could not understand this. And of course I knew the answer immediately. In the British Columbia mountains there was a panther. He was in the flowers, and a big bear was not too far off. So this big mountain lion sat there and started eating the flowers. And there was the bear in another group of flowers, and he was eating them. And then the panther ran out to frighten the bear and—whoa!—the bear just looked at him. What could attract this? There was only one thing, and that is salt. I could pull in a whole herd of deer here by putting a block of salt on a box—they can smell that for miles around. That mountain has big slabs of salt, and these animals just come for the salt, not to kill one another."

"Now, that was a big lesson to me. What would draw us together? What would pull mankind together? There, it was the salt. It was wild animals not killing one another off as they generally do. That would be the thing to work toward. Not that you would come to an answer, but you would come to a kind of suggestive way; and you would outgrow that and begin another way, because I don't think there's any real answer."

"You see, when Christianity came in, Christ was the symbol. It attracted all of Greece, all of Rome, all over. That was the catalyst. No matter how they practice, or what they did, or what they have now, it did affect a large, large group of people, whether they were Orthodox Church, Greek Church, or Roman Church. That kind of thing would be preferred. Not literal food…I think we all have to get over this idea about the starving Indians, because food isn't the catalyst. Mankind needs a shock—another kind of food. And if that came, we probably wouldn't recognize it for a few hundred years."

"I spoke of various things, and one is that I drink. I can't say that I drink objectively. Many people are upset about this, and God knows, I can say this…I didn't start drinking until the army, but it was later. In a sense, it's not to overcome something—it gets me out of the state I'm in, and you can say the same thing about drugs and things like that—it wouldn't matter to me. But I know myself on this—people do not like it."

"Now, that is not my hard luck, because I do not consider what most people think at all. It's my existence, what I wish to do. I'm out to be a normal person. I'm not out to be a person who 'surely mercy and goodness will carry me all the days of my life.' It doesn't affect me that way, thank God, it doesn't. I have no guilty conscience about anything I have ever done, or my travels around the world. I never regretted a thing. I stopped traveling. I stopped drinking. I stopped this and that and the other, and that is the time I really took stock of myself: where I am, what I'm doing, what I wish to do. How I will attempt to guide this existence with the knowledge that most things are forgotten except these man-made flaws."

"Now, I'll illustrate just once. If you say of a person: 'Oh, he's a loose person,' that sticks to him—labeled forever—forever and a day. All the rest is forgotten. Now, when it comes to this sort of thing, I don't give a hoot in hell what anybody thinks, because I graduated from that a long time ago. As I said the other night, we have lived many hundreds of lives, many kinds of lives, some, as is said, regrettable. For me, I graduated from all that—period. Because I know things about myself. Nothing is regrettable. That's what I want to say tonight. Most things are forgotten."

"Now, the thing that I mentioned last night was that no one has any idea of the kind of life that Mr. Gurdjieff led—and he led a tough, tough life. It's remembered by some of us, but hardly anything is remembered. He was a tough, tough man who lived his life fully. Not that I'm trying to copy this kind of thing, because I could never come near it. But this is my existence, and that's his, and that's yours, and that's yours! And if you hold regrets, you'd be using up forces and powers that you should be adding to yourself. Add growth to yourself instead of using it negatively— 'I should have done this, I should have done that.' Don't allow that kind of thing to enter the picture, because we inherit an awful lot of these moralistic laws. Thank God, they never existed in my tribe of Scandinavian people, but they do exist for most Americans. You'll be stopped in your tracks. Not that I'm issuing a moral statement, but you won't do anything but worry, or think and think and think. Believe me, I know—I have a few years to go, and I'm going to live them the way this creature has learned that he has to live them. In order to do something, I need that little residue that I have, the only residue that's going to be left behind. That's all, and it's finished."

"Man really works hard. We have outgrown some things. For God's sake, don't hold onto things we should cast out of our systems. We have lived a hundred lives in our lifetime, and cast them off. We can't remember what we've done, what has happened. There are many, many years of my life where I don't know one thing that happened. One thing in a year! In years! Think it over. See where you land."

"So, from now on, make the best of it, because you have a clue to answers. You are together, which makes a great, great force. And by virtue of being together, you can make a contact with one another that you can't make anywhere else, because they wouldn't understand the language or the feeling or what you're striving for as they are striving."

"Now, I've spoken two or three times to this crew, and I've spoken to the other group. I thought you had that big hanging over period, and God knows, this may be the last time I'll speak to you all for a long time because of certain conditions. I wish someone would ask something so we could all join in a kind of answer to…not a problem, but which is the big problem. Life is the problem, daily living is the problem. But we should be able to contribute something to it, not for our welfare, but for our growth. Something greater."

"One great thing, of course, is that I don't know your life, I don't know anything. I don't know if you go to other similar meetings, or if you just come to this one. If you come to this one, you know that this exists. There are ten thousand things to go to seeking solace, seeking this, seeking that, seeking everything under the sun. Now, hanging on by your fingernails and tenterhooks and whatever, you have to know this is so. Being on the periphery, and just hanging on, and slipping off, and going like this, you know that exists. Someday, within yourself—and I'm not saying this just to be funny—you'll find an answer where you have a great work, wherein it will be like a new beginning. 'Why didn't I see this before? It is beginning anew in me, it has always been around me; it surrounds me. It is everything to me, why couldn't I do that?' This is so. I've witnessed this kind of thing. Well, this'll only partially answer your question. What to do in these desperate situations? You may not come to it, frankly, until you're ready to pass out of the picture; when it may come to you, or you may come to it, in a dream. And as you say, you were thinking about it on the way here. You'll think about it later. You think about it from all angles and until that thing happens, like that!"

"The theory I live on is this: if man has done anything, if anything has ever been done, even in his aspirations—probably even in his dreams, or imagination—we should be able to do it. We should be able to conquer anything and do it. Not anything, but one thing. The hardest thing of course, the hardest thing in the world, is what we're talking about. It's our own development, and it's an impossible thing; but still it is very, very possible. You can see it in little bits and starts."

"That's the way we'll talk. We'll have an open forum. And then, I'll never say, but I do judge, as to where you are and where I am and things like that. That's the only way we can help one another, and not have the wheels going around and produce a psychological question entirely from one center. It has to be from your 'all' as closely as possible in order to grow, and we all have to grow. "

"There is a thing, now, that I thought of today about ourselves being everything. All of us contain the same thing, which is that we represent, by virtue of being born, everything that has happened and is within the whole scope of the human family, as it were, throughout the earth. We all have certain characteristics, certain lines of things, certain patterns that are mankind. You have to start thinking of very strange things sometimes. Not why am I here but why are humans here? Why is this the only planet…and why is it not?"

"The thing that we're interested now in is that we represent every vibration, as human beings, and, as I was saying, we are loved by many people and we are hated by many people. Some people think we're God-awful as an individual, and some people think we're simply wonderful. And so it goes, up and down the ladder. But never, never, never feel alone because whoever thinks that doesn't know enough."

"We represent everything, and everybody represents everything. That's why it's hellish to feel sorry for oneself. Feel sorry for what? We're all in the same boat. Some people may have a higher IQ than others, but that doesn't matter. All the arts exist in everyone, from the Bushman in South Africa right on through every tribe, every civilization, every group of people. They have this one thing we all have in common. Now, different cultures have developed it in various degrees, but they all have their own form of architecture. Even the Eskimos have their igloo. They have their sculpture, their painting, their theatre, their dance, and right on through. That's seven, and the last one, that would start a new octave, would be to enhance the ordinary aspects of all of those mentioned, so long as we don't lose ourselves completely within what is known as civilization and go off the deep end. What I mentioned as leading into a higher octave would be to attempt to do things more objectively and with the ordinary senses."

"I could talk all night, but either ask me a question or say something. Where the hell am I? What are we? It won't be a question of answering, it'll just be a question of saying something that I believe in. I'm not a teacher of any kind—it's just my own development. And I want, instead of fighting with you, instead of fighting for your development, to tell you these stories in order to be part of a whole scheme of things. That's why I give you these things."

"I'm only saying this to ask you: what do you do with your existence? Or is that too much for you? You have to go beyond what you are living in this daily life. Or doesn't that make sense? What is the recognition for you of the scriptural form of writing, and what is your recognition of the ordinary form of writing? Writing is the least of the existence. Writing is the last form that has been introduced to mankind. It's not one of the seven arts. It's not one of the natural things that have been with mankind. Every civilization—no matter where it is, whether in Patagonia or in Africa—has architecture, sculpture, all the arts, but that doesn't necessarily mean that they have to have writing. It's expressed deeply in every other way. Why do you think the whole earth is upside down, even though there have been billions of words written, almost weekly, about conditions, and no one understands? It's not the right expression, and it's not the right communication."

"If I can say it, it's the expression of a person to a person, mankind to mankind. All the vibrations exist within me and cut through your head to another person—but not through intellectual banter or the written word. If I give you Henry Adams' *Mont St. Michele and Chartres*, then your whole emotional expression can develop into something else, because it is an introduction more than a way. It introduces in quite a high form. It took Henry Adams eleven years, but before that, how did he think this out? How do you think Christ Almighty ever gathered his forces of mankind? That was his expression, but that was there, right… you understand? If you get up in the classroom, it's not what you read but what you say. It's like Abelard and Eloise. Abelard was a philosopher and Eloise was a student. This was years ago, in the eleventh or twelfth century, and he expounded the philosophy, and she was a student. It was the ancient Greek understanding of what scholasticism should be. Thousands of students used to come there to hear a person expound and they had the faculty of remembering every word that was said. And of course the great disaster was that Abelard fell in love with Eloise. Eloise was brilliant, and Abelard was brilliant beyond belief. Her uncle, the great duke of Burgundy, had him castrated. Abelard retreated to a monastery and became the bede of the order, and Eloise went to a nunnery. This was the great love of mankind. They're both buried at Père Lachaise Cemetery where they represent it. It's the most curious thing—a stone shaped like a heart in the walk."

"Where they got these things God only knows. But that is the great love story of our time, and the most tragic thing in the world. It's the most tragic love story that has ever existed. I think the recognition, as you go through your travail of research and everything, your recognition of these things, it's not to recognize Abelard, but to discover your recognition."

You, I see, I have a very strong misgiving about this word 'love,' which came through the Greek civilization. Plato expounded on 'love,' and that carried on into the Christian tradition, because the Christian religion is based on the term 'love'. If you can put it in one word, it's 'love'. And to me that's devastating, that is not true. The whole concept did not come from Christianity but from Greece. Now, why they picked on this word 'love,' God only knows. If you look at other concepts of religion, as in India, or China, they're not (based) on 'love'. They sought wisdom. And we got the emotional term 'love'. I think the whole thing will pass out; it can't exist on an emotional term. Now I'm finished talking.

In late November 1970, Mr. Benson took over his wife's groups when she fell ill. One evening her younger group came to the cottage in Mt. Kisco to met with him and he spoke to them as follows:

"We will have a short meeting on account of circumstances. I promised to be here, and I am here. I do not want to talk about psychological exercises. I do not wish to talk about psychological things. I will talk in a more tangential way, and a great deal of it you will have to figure out."

"First I have to get the idea over that the Work consists of many ways; like a wheel with a hub that has many spokes. The center of that hub you would not think was moving by the motion of the outside. The center pinwheel only moves a little bit, but it does move. It is not static. It is the core. In all exercises you will come to this hub, and the spokes are the various ways to the center. There is more than one way to reach the center of your polarity, your very life, but this is our way. This spoke is our way. There are many spokes and the motion is very great on the outside and very small in the center of the wheel. The core of truth is there. You have to seek it later. I have a theory, that by virtue of being born you are pure, you have being—and as civilization creeps in on us it [being] pours out of us. We say of children, 'They are growing up'; but they are losing their purity. I sensed this as a child, way back, about two or three years old. It is a good exercise to go back and remember some incident. Then you lose that. That is why we grow older. As they say, 'We mature.' Then we seek something-ness, that something we have lost. We can say that in this work we attempt to block this drainage, this seepage, throughout one's whole existence, and this is one of the difficult operations of understanding. We attempt to retrieve what we have lost."

"I am sure all of you have sensed, in a deep way, a sense of purity, of being, at times. Some of my great moments of existence were as a child. They were not psychological, as civilization would like to interpret them. They were real, and have stayed with me all my life."

"So I started seeking—as a child I knew better—and after the First World War I was in difficult straits. It upset me. It upset my conviction and I went round the world two or three times, seeking. That was the importance of living. It was important as a young man; I had gone through perfect hell. I did not know—not so much what to do, but what to turn to. I lived alone. I was upset, and more than upset; I was suffering deep remorse. All of us go through phases of this kind of thing. It was real. I was strong physically and in my will."

"I want to get into your thinking processes a sense of growth. How does one hold a shield to keep out the poisons, and retain what you have in order to really fight for your existence and inner growth? You know Mr. Gurdjieff would say a curious thing: 'The angels are pure, and there is no place for them to go. We on this earth are fallen angels, but we have a place to strive for, objectively and actively to come to.'"

"We dare, unconsciously, and by virtue of being here—through understanding or whatever you are. You are listening to a definite line of work, actually taking part. This is one of the objective moves you have all made, and of course, I made it many years ago, the attempt to do something with your own lives. You are taking part in a force, such as God's work. You have taken a part of God's work—great forces. You're attempting to take over your own existence. Perhaps it is not understandable. You are part of something that is very vital. It is up to you as individuals, deeply and honestly, to interpret what is happening, to you—it is always up to you. You can never be let down by any individual on the face of the earth, because you are participating in something greater, in order to grow."

"This scheme of things, in our own way, is part of a tradition. We happen to be the living objects of that tradition, and we are part of that tradition and of that spoke that leads to the center of things—the center is you as an individual. Each individual is the center, to himself, of this work. What do you think of your own lives, your own existence? And, what are you doing about it in order to grow to something? You can have this and sit there, like everybody else under the sun, by the billions, without coming to anything. There are some people who have come to something in their individuality. You are living tissue and therefore the demand is that you have to pick up and grow. And that can be. It is a movement within one's life. I read about ten books at a time, and I come upon something that is within my scope. It is within the realm of what I have set out to become, not that I know the goal. In a curious way, you grow by doing. I have been with animals all my life, but I never dared to think that it could be this way, that I had contact with animals, until it happened not too many years ago. Working in the garden, and there were four or five deer looking—one does not dare to move—and they were without fear. Also with birds. I have handled thousands of animals, and I never dared to think I had contact. I have had all kinds of animals absolutely tamed, and I never allowed myself that one thought. I can say that now. You come upon something that you really deeply feel. Otherwise you will kill yourself and not go anywhere. I could call the grouse—the wild birds."

"Then there is the other side of the subject, and that is to allow, within the whole sphere of your thinking, to allow things to happen. This is one of the stumbling blocks—we think we know better. We kid ourselves and will not allow this or that. By illustration I will tell you of when I was in France, on the way to Mont St. Michel by train. I was taking my time at the railroad station and there were two magnificent teams of horses and a carriage, and this old, old woman. On account of one's clothes people can tell you are American—and she said to me, 'I was born in Tennessee and I have not been back to America since I was sixteen. Would you come home and have chocolate with me?' She was nearly ninety. I allowed this to happen. She was the widow of the Marshall who defended Rome. She had a tremendous chapel, and a big chateau, and thousands of servants. She said, 'I go every day to the railroad and if there are any Americans I speak to them. You can stay here and tell me stories.' I said I could not. She told me I was pleasant, and that I could come back. It is an exercise I have never forgotten. Another time I went to live with a young priest in a monastery. He was being transferred and we met on the coach. I could not speak French and he could not speak English. I had brought bread and wine, and he brought wine, and we divided our spoils. And, suddenly, he insisted I go to the monastery. But I allowed it to happen, and it took me thirty-eight years to find out why. It was how I broke bread. There are orders within orders, and recognition is by various means, and this order recognized its members by the way they broke bread. I know they were watching me at the monastery. Here I was white, Protestant and Scandinavian. I know they were watching me and I was, watching them. You never know what you do in these exercises to allow things to happen, allow vital things to happen otherwise nothing will happen. You know better—you don't. Small things add up, and suddenly you recognize various things that are written. For instance, in a book written by a Danish scholar, translated into English, I came across a real pure, positive sentence. In olden days, as now, the Church was going through terrific change and Abelard was the spark. He lived through one center, and that was his brain, he gave them a hard time of it. Then he met Eloise and he became a complete animal for a time. He wrote one sentence: 'Tradition is alive only when it can inspire the creation of new life.' You can fight through the tradition, but do not live under canon law — do not split hairs about the law. We do not want to do that within our work. Fight for your existence. Fight for your life."

9 | JOHNSONTOWN

"A dog will look up to you, and a cat will look down upon you condescendingly. But a pig will treat you as his equal."

"FIRST I WENT UP and I found an isolated place in Johnsontown. You see, it all belonged to New York State, and they wanted someone, not the Johnsontowners. They knew I had arrived and they said, 'We'll build a cabin, if you help.' And I worked on it, and the Johnsontowners helped build the log cabin."

"It was hickory ... no, chestnut. All the chestnuts died after 1913. Oh, the place was full of chestnuts. I lugged the roof up from the lake on my back. You know how heavy chestnut is? I lugged and carried all sizes of boards for the roof. And finally I had the whole thing up there, and they all told me to put the roof on and tarpaper it. We chinked up all the logs and got a big stove, and that was that. I moved in. But I helped build that damn thing, and I enjoyed myself, enjoyed my existence there."

"You see, in a curious way, you know what to do, even if you don't know what to do; even if you have never done anything like it before. In these forces that exist, you know what to do, because you've been close to the natural forces for generations. You don't know, but you do know. For many generations we were close to all the natural forces. Then they came and they wanted me to shoot wild dogs. They sent Chief Gee, an Indian fighter. He was the chief of the constabulary, and he was in his seventies. But he brought over huge horse pistols from the Indian Wars, and rifles that I shot. It almost killed me, knocked me for a loop. And he said, 'I'll teach you how to shoot.' They kept after me, and they made a tremendous effort to hunt these wild dogs, because I was there. The Johnsontowners were pirates. They didn't trust them at all; they didn't want to work for the state. It was against their religion. So when I finally agreed, I think I got eighty or a hundred dollars a month."

"Then the state put in seventy-five elk from Yellowstone Park, where its forty-five below, and thought they could take that weather up there. But the elk all died of pneumonia. No animal can take this climate on the Eastern seaboard. No domestic animal can stay outside…only further South. Up in New York State, up in New England and Canada they're all in big barns. I thought the elk were all dead. We all did. And then I shot this big buck. I thought it was a big deer, but it was the last elk in the park. So I got frightened as hell and I ran. I guess I ran about eight miles. That's what you do up in that country."

"You never walk. You're like an Indian. I was always on the dogtrot. I had this damn thirty-thirty rifle with me, and I ran back to Johnsontown to tell them that I'd shot the last elk. They said, 'Where?' And I took them there and they butchered the elk, and told me I'd done the right thing. They called me 'Ben.' And they said, 'Ben, that was the right thing to do.' They never got over that—I became a hero overnight, and forever I was a hero. I wasn't a spy for the state, which they had suspected. But the state never heard about it."

"I got arrested by the sheriff once. We had a lake from which we used to harvest ice. And it was cold; my God, it was cold. The lake had a lot of floating islands that would come up. You see, it was an artificial lake, and the state thought we could kill the artificial islands with blue vitriol, so they sent two barrels, enough to kill the whole United. States. I received orders to get a rowboat, and trail one or two bags in back of the boat. It killed all of the fish in that pond and all the fish in the next pond, with the overflow. I was arrested, and everybody who gave me the orders was arrested by the sheriff."

"Living quite alone in the Ramapo hills, I had a pig, and I called this pig 'Papoose.' And you know, pigs grow; in six months they can grow to one hundred pounds and in a year they're *big*! Papoose only got what he hunted for, which was acorns, and he could grow quite quickly. We'd take long walks in the forest. We lived in a log cabin, and Papoose was just like a dog—he chased every snake out of the county, chased everything away. One day I was away. I had a tub of apple butter—we had everything in bulk—and evidently he smelled this apple butter and charged through the screen door, like that—you never saw such a mess in all your life. He just turned everything upside down, and the apple butter was all over the plantation. When I came back, there was Papoose lying sound asleep. It almost broke my heart when I had to give Papoose up, because he was so crazy. I don't know if you know, but pigs have the highest IQ of all animals. There's nothing smarter than a pig."

"Sheep are the dumbest. The sheep is stupider than anything you'll come upon. Of course a goat is very brilliant. A goat is smart as hell. But I had a saying about pigs: 'A dog will look up to you, and a cat will look down upon you condescendingly. But a pig will treat you as his equal.'"

10 | WORKING

"They want to fluctuate the truth and dismantle it."

"I THINK A PERSON IS BORN, more or less, with a desire, from the beginning, to seek, to search, and to have experiences. I've had all kinds of crazy experiences, and I benefited from them because I could understand them. Otherwise, I would just live as a vegetable, as nothingness. I believe in that theory more than the one of being reborn, even if it comes to a kind of recognition down the line. The one line that I remember from that book, *Letters To A Scattered Brotherhood*, is that the people who are killing and doing all kinds of disastrous things are the people who are still living within the ancient darkness of the race. They're still within the dark period, and they should be forgiven."

"You could stop your groups because you have had an accumulation of growth in being, not in knowledge so much, but in being. I think this is possible. I can go to only about half of the things (and I hate like hell to even leave this place), but I think that that is the progress, the growth of being more than any other thing; and you don't live with this, you just touch upon it here and there, and it becomes clearer. Therefore, you can slough off many things; all kind of ways have been attracted and distracted, all kinds of positions are in view. There is no formula."

"The Work in which we're concerned happens to be our work. We happen to be together. And there is one theme that is quite true among all of us. We happen to be here, and we happen to be thinking of this work, and how we can do better, and all the gyrations of mankind within the framework of this work. So I would like to go from there, from that picture."

"To *be* is the one really major factor of your existence, but to get there is a long travail. The body disintegrates. All kinds of things happen. But what you have developed into—that is your work. You can't go beyond that because you don't know any better. You get less of that, because you haven't worked hard and diligently towards that. It works both ways. But to be on the spot, as I am, say, tonight, because I am ill; it's worse than you think. It's the crazy thing I say all the time: 'I'm worse and I'm better at the same time, because I know this position of being on the spot.' Hot or cold, no matter what happens, I would be here talking to you all. I can make any excuse in the world. That's where your nerves are on tenterhooks, like that. Everything is out like antennae—you're receiving, and at the same time, by virtue of you all being here, there's a definite force of people. You are receiving another food for the challenge to express your truth. Deep down inside, you make that expression."

"This is our Work. As I express myself now, that is where I am. Being put on the spot is the best position to be in, and you can't just walk out of the situation and everything you have been seeking all these years. You have a sentence, a word, whole ideas that are never expressed, but through this force you can call it forth."

"I always say at Armonk, when you're dead, you're dead for a long time. Remember that, and do everything possible now, while you're alive. Some mornings, I'll stand outside and just look. Just stand and look and say to myself, 'Well, all this is living and alive, and in the course of time it outgrows itself and goes to pieces, or else it's chopped down, and we insert what we know as 'civilization,' put a road through a house and things like that.'"

"But there is this amazing thing that *does* happen, and I'm quite sure it happens. It seems to happen all the time; and that is a seed that doesn't die."

"They say they have found clover seed that is sixty years old. I always speak about this experiment I tried when we were in Washington, Connecticut on the farm. I rented a level ten-acre piece to a man who wanted to raise potatoes. He plowed it and fertilized it, harrowed, and then he planted potatoes, made rows, did everything to it. I left it after he harvested it, as kind of a shambles, in the rough. I never straightened it out or did anything. The weeds grew tall as this room, just like a big forest, and I just cut them down. The next year, smaller and different types of weeds grew in there, and I let that stay and never took it out, because the juices and the sustenance go into the soil even though they're not buried. Then the third or fourth year, the most beautiful crop of crimson clover came up out of nowhere. And here I was, amazed to see this whole field. Then I took that out."

"They took a building down in New York, and different kinds of seed plants—every damn thing—came up out of the rubble after they leveled off the street. It just grew. These weren't planted or flown in; they just lay dormant. I happen to believe that seed does not die. If anything is close to reincarnation…."

"I have a theory about this type of thing. I think some people are born with greater being than other people. They have to be educated, in a sense, not educated in a school, but 'brought out.' If they stay at it they can understand more and more and eventually become an entirely different person through that understanding. But I don't think this is acquired so much."

"The desire is to find something, reach something better. By Mme. Ouspensky staying in bed, there's not a false motion expressed. Nothing is wasted, and she can come to it. We're taking impressions in all the time; everything else is disturbing. Now I happen to know a woman out in California who's in an iron lung. She's had a few children, and the family cares for her a great deal of the time, but she doesn't even worry about the family. She has said she 'wouldn't give up this thing for anything,' because there's nothing to disturb her, nothing to take her from a line of thought, and this is very, very important."

"It's like this girl in Michigan who's paralyzed. Her father was an artist, and she could write poetry. She couldn't *write*, but she could compose poetry if someone wrote it down for her, and her father would illustrate it. He finally got together a group who did bookbinding and then bound her poetry. Every page is a different kind of paper, with some of her poetry and some of his beautiful paintings, and you can't buy the darn thing. All of them sold. She is able to do this; most likely she wouldn't be able to do it if she was normal."

"We went to Yom Kippur, and that was a remarkable experience for me, because the Rabbi, who was from Germany and had gone through the war, said the most marvelous things. He said, 'All people have attitudes regarding every thing, but seek that attitude that is within you. All people have an atmosphere, and there is a great atmosphere about us. But seek that atmosphere within you. We all think we have great authority regarding other people. And this is quite true. But seek that great authority within yourself and not through exploiting other people.' They were the most marvelous words I have heard for one hell of a long time."

"I think most likely it's my thoughts that are invading the situation. Wherein I don't give a damn. Not that I say I think. Who thinks? Who is in possession of their faculties? That is my big worry. I wish I was. I want to be. And that's the terrible thing. I'm dying on account of that. It's that I'm not in possession of what is within me. Every book I read—I'm impressed. It's not the reading, and it's not what one remembers in reading. This is what I go through almost every night: *You're a living creature*, and why are you in such a quandary of seeking to know? I don't want to read about it. The fight has to be the big fight with oneself through the understanding of what you're thinking about. Through that understanding you may gain knowledge; and there is your attempt, the only attempt you have. The only possibility is to grow, to grow into a sense of being. Nothing else exists—not the reading, not the interpretation. I could read millions and millions of books. I have, and that doesn't make me any better. You are either the *crucified* or the *crucifier* of immoral indignation of this civilization today."

"I think in a curious way, people years ago had clever minds, but they were not fast thinkers. This is a crazy theory of mine, because it doesn't happen to me, that I can, as I think things through and start writing it. It's no good. Take a person like Gorham Munson. He was a slow conversationalist. But in that tempo he was able to retain his thoughts and write them out as fast as they happened. Mine are gone when I start writing. I know I have missed some points and I can't retrieve them. So I always thought maybe they're slow enough to express it. It's the most curious thing. I have a good line of thought and when I start writing it, it withers. Not on a big subject, but on emphatic little things. They don't happen that way to me. Like Mr. Gurdjieff wrote this whole god-damn book of millions of words and had the whole thing in mind. And, that's something else again, when you have a big subject in mind, you know you can approach it from many, many angles. But when there's no subject in mind, and then you write little things…the main subject is your own self, your own development. Then you have to write, if you write, something towards that end…but then its in the wilderness all the time."

"A lot of things have to be done when a person is inspired. And to what end? Not that the end is seen, but they're going towards something. Orage used to give talks on this kind of thing…about writers…and he said, "Even constipation will affect people." Anything…you can tell right down the line; all kinds of things. When my wife was in the hospital, and I was distressed, I could no more think of writing than flying a kite, or putting anything down. It didn't matter. I think the idea of inspiration and if it could be done at that time. It's not like newspaper reporting where the day is the subject. It's a curious thing with the forms of writing; what do you write for? Why does a person want to write? And there are many, many arguments about that. Of course to affect people, the highest form of writing is scriptural writing, which is done in simple forms. All religious writings are done in simple form. It's the composition that really makes the effect. It's the way the thing is constructed. And the subject is always man's salvation, no matter how you look at it and that kind of affects people. It's affected people for thousands of years. Now we can't go to the highest form of writing, because writing has been reduced to all kinds of things."

"Oh, boy, they hate me like poison. I'm the nigger in the wood-pile, and God knows I'm putting myself on the spot in every way. Not only now, but all my life…to know some truth, to know something of the truth. They will not allow themselves to put themselves on the spot. They want to fluctuate the truth and dismantle it. Well, there's only one approach for me, and that is to be absolutely honest to myself and to whomever I'm dealing with, whether they recognize it or not."

"That condition is one that every religious group is striving for. I don't think we have the possibility of reaching consciousness. But I often thought of these episodes of mine and then reading about them in our language in a simple, simple way. They're very simple books. You may think me absolutely crazy for thinking that they are something, but I recognize two or three things that were within this area. And I think, in a strange way, that we're raised to believe that it's only the heavy tomes that are the real books, like going in to read all the philosophers like Kant, or Kepler, and it isn't so. People's education has been delved into by every philosophy, of heavy, heavy-laid things. Kant had some very good things; things that I remember, anyhow. I'll read some of those to you sometime. They're marvelous. Then you skip miles. But it isn't necessary, that's the curious thing. This awareness that we speak about or talk about—I told you some time ago that I recognized this in very simple forms, even in the writings of Knut Hamsun. A boy who had no contact with anything—just a wild kid up in Norway—suddenly heard the wood duck call. It was a thing that has existed for millions of years, but *he* heard it. And that was the beginning of his development: to hear something."

"I told you about this curious thing that's happened to me. Of course, I don't want anybody to hear of this kind of thing, and the possibility exists that this could happen…. And now, the way I feel I'll allow it to happen. This is one of my strange philosophies. I'm always preaching to allow things to happen to you, to everybody. But when it came to this…I wouldn't allow it to happen, more or less."

"I decided in the last two years. Things come in a very slow way, in a very slow fashion over hundreds of years, thousands of years. I think it's the way our heredity is. If things like that happen to me, I'm going to allow them."

"I have heard the sound. It wasn't seeing anything and I was absolutely aware of the people about me, but I wasn't there. That's why I sit at the table because I can put myself in a position as if I'm above looking down on the whole gang. Now this I can't do all the time. But this is my attempt. And I can feel, like that's the bigger arc of vision. As if I'm looking down and yet be a part of the whole community that way, instead of just looking. There is a hell of a big difference in what I'm saying than just sitting straight and staring out."

"These are some of the so-called mysteries that are never spoken of, but when people go to sittings they are attempting something of this order, to be a part of themselves and to be so completely a part. You don't hear the tone completely, but you hear the echo. You hear the echo of that tone. That describes that situation much better than I can point it out to you. I heard the echo. I heard Olga de Hartmann's voice saying, "Martin, Martin"—just a faint, faint thing—and I said to myself, 'They're calling me.' This is true. I'm telling you something that's absolutely true. I stopped conversing between Mme. de Salzmann and Bill Segal, and suddenly ... like that. It's a form of consciousness, not a form of unconsciousness. You hear, but you hear the echo of the thing."

"The Old Man had things to say when he used to send us to the church: 'You get yourself into an objective state and you steal their prayers.' If I had gotten into a state like that at Saint Eustache and Notre Dame, sitting alone in the back and listening to the beautiful music and the prayers, I could have captured those prayers. He said, 'You steal their prayers, because you need them for your growth ... because they haven't got the power to reach their God.' Now, if I was in a state as I mentioned, I could have stolen those prayers, but I have never been. But that was an exercise of that order. It is one of the reasons, on account of these conditions and on account of knowing this, that, and the other thing, that I adhere to the Work. At the same time, I'm not afraid of a living soul, because I know all the ideas of a hierarchy, and so it's like the Catholic Church."

"They're frightened to death of a vision or a miracle happening, because they have to do all kinds of somersaults to be approved, and they don't want that. They don't want miracles. But when it does happen, they can't do anything about it. It isn't a question of the hierarchy of the church approving a miracle, and that's why they don't want to have anything to do with it. It didn't come through the hierarchy, cardinals and bishops and down the line: 'Oh, you have a miracle!' So I never talk about these things, or anything like this to anyone, only people who were there, Because they did happen, and I'm still living, and I don't think I'm off my rocker."

"Then I stopped the whole thing. And I think it did me a world of good to stop, because I went into the farming in a very big way, with gusto and keeping *this* animal healthy. That's why I say I know I could help Bill Segal. I'm not near him, but if he comes out, I could give him strength, because I'm healthier than he is now. I can afford many things because I understand this. I don't think he understands that. For him to go off alone on a spiritual jag is not going to be any good. He has to strengthen his body. That's why I said to him, 'You go live in a slaughter house. Regain your strength.'"

"You know who was in that state, many, many times and for a long time, was the Maharashi. [Sri Ramana Maharshi] Now he was born the way he was and he longed to get out of the whole earth. I don't do that because I confess I had certain fears about the whole thing—a lack, a real lack of understanding. I was within the power of something, but it was never fully explained. And I didn't trust any manuscript or reading. I knew it was absolutely different. Any book, anything you pick up, has this kind of thing. That's what they're striving for. When it happens, what do you do? A great deal is that you have faculties and conditions in your makeup and what you have inherited that is just right for certain things. It's like perception. Many people have perception in greater degrees than others. But to think, as the modern scientists now say: 'Well, that's a part of schizophrenia.' Well, who the hell knows. I think all of those people, all those doctors, are the schizophrenic people. Most of them are. And who knows."

"These phases go through one like a flash, and one is able to sit down and do this kind of thing. It's not constant with me; I have days. Every week I have days when I'm hitting some high spots. It's never entirely lost, but it isn't on all the time. When I don't sleep, and when I lie awake in bed, delving into things, and I come upon some really marvelous ideas that I know will be gone if they're not written or said because I'm more or less half asleep. One is not fully awake, and therefore one can dismiss many things. I think a great many crimes are committed when people are half there, like a policeman who killed his wife and said, 'I killed her because I loved her.' You do vital things in a somnolent state."

"At Mendham one time I could get into a state, and I forcefully stopped doing that. In the beginning it was not brought on; I didn't will it. But later I could, and then I stopped. I thought it would be too damned dangerous a position. Say, we were sitting at a table, and I was sitting opposite Mme de Salzmann. It was a double table, and I think Segal was sitting beside me. We were eating and we were talking across the table, and suddenly I was out of it—just like that, out of the whole conversation. I was not there. Then I heard Mme. de Hartman calling, 'Martin, Martin ....' And I said to myself, I can remember that's Mme. de Hartman calling me, and I was not in this presence. Then I came out of it, and Mme de Salzmann looked at me, and she said, 'Can you tell me where it was where you were now?' It was probably half a minute. Olga kept yelling, and I could hear her. Later on this happened where I could just go out. It wasn't any subject that brought this on; it just happened. And I knew it happened, that was the thing, I knew I wasn't there. I knew I wasn't conscious of being there. I knew I was conscious of something else. This happened a couple of times, and then I knew I could more or less, in a sense, will this, and when that happened then I stopped."

"Frankly, I don't know why I thought it was dangerous. If I had been alone, I wouldn't have felt it was dangerous, but there were about eighty people in the room. I wasn't facing them, but I knew I was not there. And it wasn't a kind of self-hypnosis. We were talking, and suddenly I went out like that—wide awake."

What did you answer Mme de Salzmann when she asked you?
"I said, 'I was far, far away. I was not here, except I could hear Olga calling as if she was whispering. And I said to myself, 'There's Olga calling me.' Not across the table, but like a whisper.' I don't know what the hell it was. I never delved into it, but I was conscious of many, many things. I've often thought of that. You know why I don't go to sittings? On account of that. That's what people want to get into, and here it's not a stumbling block for me. I've witnessed that a number of times. I always tell Mme. de Salzmann, 'Well, I'm not

ready to go to sittings. When I don't feel ready, I won't go.' But I just don't go, anyhow. I don't know if I can tell you this, but the reason people go to sittings is the thing I don't want to go to sittings for. I defeat myself in this thing. Now that possibility exists with me."

"Now, if I was with the Old Man, who was an authority on this, I could see what the danger could be or if that is the state. I've been warned about this—we were warned. Instead of arriving at a state of absolute awareness of yourself—what we call consciousness—you may arrive at what we call illumination. This is what the Japanese go in for in Zen. The danger of a process is that one could go so far and never return. At the same time I know this is what we're striving for, in a sense. And I don't want to excuse myself, because I know I'm putting up a barrier there."

"You cannot stay only on this Work because there are many paths to the core, to the hub. There are many paths, all going in the same direction but this happens to be our path. To some, for anybody to deviate from the path, my God it is death! Well I do; because there's nobody to teach me otherwise. There's no teacher. And I know more than they do. And I sense more than the whole works. And so I delve into various things. I don't delve into the Buddhist thing because I don't understand what the hell they're talking about. Frankly I don't delve into the Zen thing because I figured out years ago they they're out after illusion not consciousness. And that I steer clear of a great, great deal, not that I steer clear, I just haven't got time. If I have time to read, I want to … you know it comes in waves. I want to read, what I want to read … what I think is that important."

"I mentioned something like this to Mme de Salzmann. You know it is not the life that a person has led, but I do think it's the interests. It's the enthusiasm that makes the life. People have lived more bitter lives, more joyous lives, more hopeful lives, more loving lives, than this one or that other person. But it's the enthusiasm that they put into that life that could affect say an autobiography. I mean, people have done such odd things."

"There was a report years ago that at times they would find Lincoln in quite a state; the same thing with William James. William James would be found in quite a curious state, and while in that state he was impossible, or everything was impossible. We think people are probably crazy, but it isn't necessarily so. A person approaching consciousness probably would be considered crazy. Now, William James, after he was in this state, would come out and everything was broken up in pieces. That's what I think about lunatics: everything is broken up. There's no connection. But, after these states, William James came out of it and was able to write these remarkable things. Lincoln, as well."

"I was born with a greater possibility than a hell of a lot of people and I accept that. There are many things that annoy me, there are many things I don't say a damned word about, things, I don't mention even to my wife, because I have this feeling that it's happening, probably in gradations, to everybody. Like when I discovered, when I was seven, eight years old, that all people didn't have true tone pitch, I was shocked. Things like that shocked me. I wouldn't dream of stopping sittings, but for me, I have to think twice."

"This Work is a very powerful work. And one of the many, many things I'm stuck with is the void. It's like steps and steps and steps, going up a ladder and daring to look over a high cliff, and seeing one's self. What do you see? A whole void. I've been stuck on that for some years. Do I fill up this void, or is the void empty and we have to fill it up by virtue of being born and living life? In context with this, delving into this, that's why many things have no value to me. There are many things that people value which really have no value, because I know, in a curious way, they can be had. Anybody can have anything or everything, but still nothing. That is a very curious way of looking at things. But is the void full and I can't see it? I can't make out the various things until I unfold this little package or that thing, by a deeper insight. It may be full. But I've been stuck on this kind of thing... I think I've had a shock in it."

"Mendham, you see, wasn't the first time. This had happened years ago. And then I really watched and became frightened, because I didn't know what the hell this was. Then, at some of the sittings, I felt as though I was not allowing room for something to enter. To put it another way, I was not allowing a space 'outside,' so I stopped. If I had allowed a space, I could go to it."

"Now, if you're involved with other people, and you're in a great battle all the time, these things won't happen to you, but you're not allowing a spot in your whole makeup for those people to be part of your life. So I stopped, and this is what's kept me in great wonderment."

"With this kind of sense, it's nonsense unless you understand what I'm talking about. It's utter nonsense, but it makes a great deal of sense for me because it's affected my whole existence. This is the big danger, and my fear is most likely groundless, but I wouldn't allow myself to get into that position. That's why I always say, 'Keep your feet on the earth.' I never talk about this to anybody. Not even God."

"I've seen Mme. de Salzmann develop. I've known her for many, many years. And I've seen her slowly and slowly and slowly…and there doesn't seem to be anything fazing her. And the other day we were rushed about this, that and the other thing in the hospital and I took her out and I said to her, 'Don't let anybody run your life—but nobody.' And she said, 'Fear not—no one is my going to run my life!' She knew what I was talking about without anything being said directly. I think when a person like Mme de Salzmann gets into a position of work, that is not only major, but she won't allow little things to come in and interfere and eat her as little things eat us up. It's not big things that eat us up. A person can be caught by many people. And you can consider people are the piranhas and take chunks out of you here and there until you just disappear, without doing one thing for yourself.

Now that's why we have these gatherings, these meetings. And they're attacked in different ways."

"Leave a whole vibration dangling, and there it is, unfulfilled, unsettled. But you have to come to your own instruction. Your own! And that's the secret of that whole damn thing. You're never lonely, because you're working out many, many problems all the time, without bitterness, without hatred; otherwise, you stop your work. It can be done, and the most challenged person in the world is myself. It hasn't been easy to figure out my way as I have figured it out. I'm following a definite line. If the people in the ice house group don't show enthusiasm, I get rid of them and get new people. Not that they have to believe in me, but they have to give toward a vibration down there, and they do. They just love the whole atmosphere. And that's very good, on account of certain demands. I don't demand anything, least of all the finished product—or to do things neatly, correctly. That's not the demand. I make such demands of the natural forces that make their senses vibrate and grow close to nature in the greater sense of the word, to actually feel that they're alive in order to do better things."

"No organization is going to teach you anything like that. You have to arrive at these things, by hook and crook, and under pressures and all kinds of fallacies you have to wade through. I know a hell of a lot regarding all the different religions, but I don't know a hell of a lot when they become a project. I get the knowledge in another way—an entirely different way. I know a great deal about Judaism, about the Moslems, about Zen. There's a marvelous book about how a monk has to prepare himself, which is very remarkable to me."

"They'd pick out a monk, and he was asked to prepare himself to make a sculpture that would fit a doorway or a niche. He would prepare himself, and think out every detail of what he was sculpting, get it into his whole being. He would isolate himself until this was finished, never report, never see a living soul. And then word was given that it was finished, and they'd investigate it, measure the space where it would go, and they would make judgment: good, bad or indifferent. And that's the place."

"The thing is, I said something last night, and what I was really thinking of was how much we really forget. Most things are forgotten in this world. You understand, even things that are written down, people don't even read them. They're just stacked away. And probably in four or five hundred years, someone will rake something up from the Congressional Record, but nothing is remembered. And you don't want to live on that basis. Know that this is so—know it."

"The thing is you can remember back to say when I started these books. This is exactly what I was trying to get at. That you have to, not grow crooked, like that girl, because she has something to straighten out, or straight, but you have to fill yourself, through your own efforts, with knowledge, in order to understand, and in order to grow; and that's how you retain it. You have absorbed something that is with you. You have absorbed it even though you don't think about it for a long, long time—many, many times. Now that's answering your question backwards, because I didn't want to forget that point; how you hold on to what you get. You hold on to what you get by deeply taking it in when you're affected."

"You know, every night I have a little say to myself, every night when I go to bed, and that is, 'Go forth'…this is biblical…'replenish the earth and subdue it.' And I hate like hell to see the way they're subduing the earth. All mankind—and this is supposed to be our advancement."

"Do you understand the situation you have to get yourself into to break these terrific happenings? That will take up a phase of your whole existence. It's there, to be placed here and be part of you, though not forever. You take on another aim. But nothing is forever. Not that you forget, but you won't put it as the major happening of your existence. Everything is moving all the time. If it doesn't move it's no good. And I'll always end up with that same thing that has affected me, and that is about tradition."

"We can live this tradition but do not live the canon law, as they call it, of the tradition, because the Roman Catholic Church split hairs over canon law instead of about their religion. We can do the same thing with our tradition—split hairs over what I call canon law instead of developing, using the tradition as a source of surprise, but not the law. You are the law. You are the judge. There are certain objective basic laws, but you are within yourself. I always say this thing about tradition that Abelard said: 'Tradition is alive, when it can inspire the creation of new work.' I think that's the most marvelous sentence I've ever heard—not a negative word in it, nothing about what *not* to do. 'Tradition is alive when it can inspire the creation of new work.'"

11 | *THE OLD MAN*

"I see Mr. Gurdjieff sitting on the moon just watching, looking at the whole universe and this earth."

"I COULD TELL YOU A LITTLE STORY in order to show you what I mean. In February of a certain year, Mr. Gurdjieff left New York for France. I saw him at the boat and told him I would be over most likely in the spring. In April I wrote to him and said I would be there the middle of April. Mr. Gurdjieff had someone send a telegram to me, saying, 'DO NOT COME, I DO NOT WISH TO SEE YOU.' I worked my way over to Antwerp as a seaman and then descended upon Paris. I had sent a telegram, 'I AM ON MY WAY.' And someone met me at the train in Paris. This person said, 'He really does not want you to come!'"

"The next day I appeared at the Prieuré and made sure Mr. Gurdjieff saw me. He said, 'Oh, you have come.' I said, 'Yes, I have come.' That evening at supper Mr. Gurdjieff found some difficulty to make use of and he said to me, 'You have to leave right away.' I left and again made sure he saw me leave. I stayed in Fontainebleau for the night and the next day I appeared at the gate. Then Mr. Gurdjieff talked to me. He said, 'I believe deeply you wish to stay—but this is a crazy place and you may not like it.' Then he said, 'Stay.'"

"After I'd been there a week, many responsibilities were given to me, and from that I felt sure that he knew he could trust me to a point, and he could pile on responsibilities. All I have told you about my getting to the Prieuré in order to stay and all that was put in the way was only to test the strength of my wish, and this was more or less how he went about it."

"There is a massive story that no one dares touch upon, and that is the real story of Gurdjieff's life. You see, everybody has a story of Mr. Gurdjieff—Olga [de Hartman] has a story, and I have one, and my wife has her particular impression. But aside from personal impressions, there is the story of his existence. There are many, many things we have to agree upon. And that is never mentioned, never. Oh, boy, talk about blood and thunder. And the women ...."

"You know, here we had two very tough hombres, Gurdjieff and Ouspensky. Gurdjieff was a natural; I think he was born that way. And Ouspensky was his pupil, after which he left Gurdjieff and never allowed one of his students, not one, to ever mention the name of Gurdjieff. Because he wanted that glory. What a heel he must have been. He died in 1947, and Mme. Ouspensky had his writings published. The book wasn't to be called *In Search of the Miraculous*, but the publishers changed it."

"Well, it doesn't matter. The thing was the Old Man died in 1949. Now Mme. Ouspensky was a power with Ouspensky there, even though she was bedridden for years. She wanted to stay in bed and be the center of attraction. You could never get near her, whatever the women said. They used to tell me, 'Now you walk in.' But try to get by five women who are guarding the door. And I said, 'No, you send for me.' But as soon as the two men died, five women took over. So I suggested last year, 'This is not the Gurdjieff Work anymore. We should change the name from the Gurdjieff Foundation to the British Ouspensky People in America Foundation.' Well, Mme. De Salzmann almost died when I said that. That's why I'm in a fury, but what the hell, I really don't care deeply, so long as nothing happens to my wife. She's worked too hard all these years for anything to happen with these bastards."

"This is what I told you before: how I had to come to that. That's what I believe in the end everyone has to come to. You just can't be a power with nothing. Power isn't registered. The only real power is for a person who arrives at an understanding with enough knowledge and background for a sense of being. The sense of being will be felt by everyone and then you are, more or less, a person who has arrived at something, no matter how small, that could be a force. Outside of that there isn't any force. Appointments are no force. And of course you don't get all your knowledge from one source, because then it's not only lukewarm, it's warped if you only stick to one theme."

"No, what I'd like to do is write about this Work, seeing as how everybody is writing. I want to give my expression and impression, and tell how I loved the Old Man and believed in him. Ask yourself sometime, how many people do you actually believe in? By knowing such a thing, it doesn't matter who believes in you. It doesn't bother me in the least. But there are a few things that have to be adhered to, that I have to follow, and one is that the story has to be honest and truthful, as I am naturally honest and truthful."

"I don't know if you know that. But I know that about myself. I'm pretty naive about many, many things, or gullible. Telling things, in the end. I'll sometimes ask myself, should I have said that? And then I think why the hell should I care? I'm living tissue and alive. Why should I care what I said? That is probably more truthful than anything that I've ever said. So I don't worry about that. That's my attack on Saturdays with the young people who have never heard anything like the things I tell them. Some of them have only been in psychological work. One of them said, 'Now I'm all mixed up. I don't know what Mr. Benson means.' Well, why the hell should he? You think I ever knew what Mr. Gurdjieff meant? Not that I'm trying to make a riddle of things, but that's the way I am. I know they have a hell of a time because I shock them. I jump from one thing to another in a big shock, in a wave and not in small, psychological sequences. That's all I'm good for, is to give out shocks. If they make reason and sense of it … they do, many of them do."

"The one thing that kept the Old Man very straight was memory, and he told me that when he was hurt in that first accident in 1924, 'Frankly I was unconscious.' He was unconscious for days. Christ, I thought he was dead. They found him across the road with his shoes off beside him. He had taken his shoes off and he was sitting on the opposite curb. The police found him. But he said, 'The one thing... the one thing was that I remembered myself.' I think the shock was so great that, probably, not realizing, he took his shoes off as if he were going into a mosque or a temple, because that was the habitually respectful thing to do. This guy was unconscious and maybe near death. I swear he was dead, for days and days. And he pulled through. Because I know when he came out to have the men cut the trees down, he wasn't talking at all. He was taken out in a wheelchair and had the men cut trees down and dig up roots at all hours of the night. He sat there to absorb the life of the trees for his physical welfare. He knew how to absorb life. It was necessary to become stronger in order to get life, to become enriched and stronger. He knew how to take this force from live trees."

"Then, I swear, he used people, the lives of people. He'd get into the middle of the Café de la Paix with all the emotions and everything going to hell while he was writing. We didn't know at the time, but later on I figured it out. He was always sitting, like Toulouse Lautrec in a brothel. He sat right in the middle with all this life—mostly Americans—and emotions and joviality, and whatever—all wasted emotions. He was writing *Beelzebub*, and I would swear he would steal these emotions because they were going wild and astray, just going out into the atmosphere. He knew how to steal their wasted emotion. He had that kind of force. That sounds so crazy, but I swear he knew how to do that. Where else could he get his strength from, except the taste of all people? He never mentioned it, but I figured it out from what he said I had to do. He said, 'The waste of emotions, the waste.... Get among crowds of people.' He said, 'The best crowds to be among were among the holidays, the holy days, of Christmas. You go to the cathedral, and you get yourself into as objective a state as you possibly know, and you steal their prayers.'"

"I used to go to Saint Eustache. You know, by the market. They had the most wonderful choir in all France. It was an unfinished cathedral. I sat and listened and tried to get into an objective state in order to take their prayers. And he approved. He said, 'You take their prayers for your development, your welfare, your strength, because they are going to waste. They have not the force, or power or understanding to reach their God.' That was the message. He said, 'They could reach their God if they knew how.' Then he told me, 'You have the wish to reach your God. It comes from you, and as you develop you can reach your God. And then you take strength from your God or from that force and take it back to you. It's like this: [*here Benson would place his hand ten or twelve inches in front of his chest and then bring it in toward his heart, in a gathering motion, several times over*] that's the motion. It has to start from you, though. Begin as the desire, the wish, and then, religiously, you study that in order to reach something higher and greater forces—in order to bring it back to you.'"

"Now, that was as practical as hell to me at one time. I had no qualms about it. And now I find myself more or less frightened to even talk about it. I won't tell the young people a thing like that because they won't understand one goddamn word. This book could have been written in houses of prostitution, and cafes and dirty dance halls and any damn place, and that's where he got the strength from, where there was life."

"I see Mr. Gurdjieff sitting on the moon just watching, looking at the whole universe and this earth. And that's where I put him: looking down on the whole fallacy of mankind, on this earth, and sending various emissaries from various planets to this earth. That's the way I see the Old Man. I see him sitting on the moon and just watching, watching the whole thing. Because it's a part of the earth. They go off to various places, and emissaries come to the earth. This is the conclusion I've come to regarding him."

"Now, the point is, what do you arrive at? What do you come to in your thoughts? You have to think as objectively as possible, and not in subjective terms. To me, the Old Man was a great man. How great I will never know. But I knew he was able to gather forces from other people that were wasted forces. I almost know this. For me he was a great, great man for being able to do that."

"Not that he was holy or anything like that. He had this force. That's why I say think of the ephemeral force, because this is an ephemeral force. You can't prove this kind of thing. He was a great man in that sense. You see, I have a theory: In a curious way, there is a Jesus Christ living, and it's not a person so much as a polarity that this has to be. This curious polarity has to be in order to hold this earth together. Now, various things can change. The form can change, but the force is always there. Always remember that: The force exists. The force is always there. I don't think there has been only one curious Jesus Christ. In that sense they do exist on the face of the earth, somewhere. No matter if the expression comes out of them or not, they do exist. And that's all I'm trying to do. I feel there has to be that kind of thing in existence at all times, and their food is mankind—their 'food' comes from mankind. When mankind passes out, they'll pass out. There's force, someone being born with this kind of structure. You see, the terrible thing is to believe that things existed only once. They have existed many, many times. There's a repetition of existence as much as there's a repetition of being born—living, and dying, the great expressions. That's why I mentioned the various civilizations; there have been civilizations beyond our capacity of knowing they existed; where great things have happened, and very awful things have happened all at once. And the big fallacy is of course, if we haven't heard about it, it never happened. This is one of the human failings. You'll hear, even today, 'Oh I never heard of such a thing'; and to them it never existed. But in a larger scale many things have existed that we have never heard of, never seen. The whole of existence has existed time and time and time again. You should believe in that kind of thing. That this isn't the first time it's happened. Believe me there have been worse times and there've been better times. But it has happened throughout the whole civilization of mankind."

"I thought when I lived at the Prieuré that I was an orphan. I used to ask Mr. Gurdjieff questions and he'd say, 'Oh....' He'd throw me aside like that. Or, when I insisted, he would come back a week later or two weeks later and say, 'You haven't come to that; no matter what I would say you would never guess it.' So then I stopped and I felt like hell. One day, arguing on the telephone (we argued every day on the telephone, we couldn't understand each other) and I said something, and he said, 'I'm coming right out and we will have coffee,' for no reason at all. Now, what I said, I don't know. I have no idea, but he knew. We went up to his room and had coffee, and he spoke to me for about two and a half hours, answering my question. And here I felt like such a heel, thinking, 'I was forgotten, I can't get anyplace, I can't do anything until I know that answer,' until I had grown into something where I could understand an answer like that."

"He told me the whole work. He said, 'You were not ready for that particular answer.' It was something vital to me. I don't know what it was. But that's the kind of position I would find myself in, and still hanging on and slipping off. You feel it in the atmosphere, people know, you feel stupid, and nothing happens. Then he said, 'You stay with me, you stay close to me and just ask questions, because you're over this thing.' Whatever it was, whatever my stumbling block was, he understood it, and he came right out in the car and drove right back seventy-five miles."

"The one big thing for me about Mr. Gurdjieff was that I believed in him. I had absolute trust and faith in him, because in my search I was looking for someone I could trust, and I came upon it. And when I came upon it, I recognized it enough to believe in it. When he told me, 'I'll teach you how to do plumbing,' I believed him. You know, I followed the principle. He told me, 'You do the plumbing,' he said. I said, 'I know nothing about it.' He said, 'I'll teach you.' And when he was teaching me he said, 'It's like your body; think of your body that has supply (first force), drainage (second force) and ventilation (third force); those three things. Now you have to learn the mechanics.' Isn't that wonderful? That's what I mean when I say I believed in him, so emphatically, no matter what."

"There is a photograph taken at our wedding, with Mr. Gurdjieff. I haven't seen it for years. He stands in between us, hanging onto us and laughing like hell. It's the only picture in the world where you see him laughing. My wife is in a long, long dress from that period, 1934. I want to find that, too."

"Did I tell you the story of that wedding? We went up with Muriel Draper to find a little church in Stamford—it's a little white church, Unitarian or Universalist—because Orage was married there. And then I found out Larry Morris was married there too. We got to the church, and we thought we could get married —we were that stupid. And the minister said, 'Oh, no, we have to have it registered, a week or ten days grace in the City Hall. Here are the forms and you can sign it and register right away.'"

"So the next week came, and we called up City Hall—it would be a week on Sunday. And they said, 'No, it's not ten days yet,' and my wife says, 'Well, it's a week.' And the woman said, 'Well, if you want to be registered as a blemished bride. It's marked on that record. Forever it's on that record.'"

"And we decided that the Old Man would be there that week, and we invited about fifteen people—Lincoln Kirstein, who was in charge of the American Ballet, and Muriel of course, and Mrs. Breslow and her mother, Miss Bentley, and Mrs. Yandel who lives in Stamford. She was my great friend. She was a little, sharp woman with black eyes, and she came in and sat right in the front row. As we got ready and walked down the aisle—there was music, the minister was ready—we couldn't find the Old Man. We didn't know where he had gone. So we had to wait. And suddenly he just walked in, just came in. He was out looking around. When the minister asked what his relation to us was, he said, 'I father both.'"

"And Mrs. Yandel jumped up and grabbed a hold of my wife as soon as we were married, and said, 'Mrs. Benson'—my wife hadn't been called Mrs. Benson yet—'I want you to understand that Ben is a part of our family, and we love him, and you had better take good care of him.'"

"Then we took over the Bedford Green Inn, and we had lunch. Prohibition had just ended with an edict from Roosevelt, so we were able to buy four bottles of vodka. My doctor was along because I had been seriously ill. He drove us up, and he took these pictures. He has one, right in the entrance of his apartment. And people always say, 'Oh, you're the one in that picture.' So, by God, for some reason or other, I have a contact with the Old Man, through many, many things."

"After we were married, we bought a place. He used to come up there to the place we rented in Woodbury, and of course, we had a wonderful time. We had a maid, and he'd chase her out and do all the cooking himself. He loved to cook, but he cooked enough for an army and there were only a couple of us there. We let him do anything. That's when I went to the Russian village with him."

"There was a Tolstoy village near Newtown. It was fenced in and had a gate, and I found out they had a printing press, and I asked him if he wanted to go. My wife and I drove him over, and he spoke Russian to them. It was Tolstoy's nephew or something. And he said, 'I think we can have *Beelzebub* published there.' And he almost made a deal. You couldn't control him."

"Then one day he had these *Herald of Coming Good* books that were written while I was at Prieuré. He had them in Russian, English and Spanish, cases of them with him. Fred Leighton had some, and Donald had some. Fred had the Russian ones, so Mr. Gurdjieff said to call up Leighton and have him bring up two boxes. I called up Fred and told him to get a certain train and I'd meet him, and he could take the next train back. I got the two cases and put them in the car and drove back, and the next day we drove up to the Russian village with a case, and I took out a mass of them in my arms."

"We had to climb this long hill, in the cold October rain, and we slipped all the way up. He went ahead, and I followed with these books. There was a line of cabins up the hill, and at each cabin he knocked on the door, and said in Russian,

'Will you please read this?' I gave him the books one book at a time, and he gave them away, going from one cabin to the other. I'll never forget that."

"He gave them out himself. His point was, as he said, 'All those who are in the Work have to pay for the printing of *Beelzebub*.' And we did pay, we all paid four hundred dollars. We had to pay for the publishing, and then we gave them away. Talk about a new idea! He said, 'We all have to go around with copies and give them to the people on the streets of New York.'"

"I can just see myself on Fifth Avenue and Forty-Second street, saying: 'Will you please read this?' and handing them out. That's the way it was going to be, and we would have done it. He didn't give a damn how much it was going to cost. We had to pay for it because we were the only ones responsible. We were in the Work. He couldn't ask for money for that. That's the way that was supposed to be done. It made life interesting. It was a kind of a shock every goddamn moment."

"There's another story, a funny one. We never understood it. Mr. Gurdjieff was on the way to Brighton Beach, on the boat, to see the Whitcomb's. They went to pick him up, but he rode out, and he said his wallet was stolen and he lost his passport. I'd like to see anybody rob him, because he was aware of everything going on all the time. I said, 'How did it happen?' He said, 'I don't know, but I have to report.' And somebody had to report to immigration. I think he threw the damn thing overboard. I never could understand how anyone could rob him. I think he threw it out, just to see what we would do."

"They put him on Ellis Island, with all these immigrants, and especially Rabbis, who came from here and there. And he had a wonderful time. Now, what values do you consider? When I look at the remarkable men, there are a hell of a lot of people I wouldn't say were remarkable at all. To say you had a whale of a time on Ellis Island…."

"He wanted to see what we would do. Well, what we did was the wildest thing. Donald Whitcomb had graduated from college with [Jerry] Voorhis's son, who was a congressman in Washington. Someone else knew a senator, and we all got in touch until we got word saying; 'Don't have anyone try to force the immigration department because they'll suspect something, and it'll make it worse.' So we had to lay off the pressure on Washington. And they let him out after a couple of weeks there, most likely investigating. But then we had to get him a passport."

"Oh, it was wild living, you know. I think he was pulling one stunt after another. What a life of excitement! Peggy Flinsch went through that; my wife went through that; and I went through it. It was very curious with Donald; he had such a feeling about the Old Man. I was in Oregon when he died, and Donald was staying with my wife in our apartment, and he wept for three solid days. And my wife called up—we were in touch by telephone all the time—and she said, 'Donald can't seem to get over that Mr. Gurdjieff died.' Then Donald retreated and wasn't ever much a part of the Work at all. But he still is in his way, but never a part of this organization."

"You see, when the Old Man died, everything died with him for Donald. I thought he would die, too. He couldn't accept that Mr. Gurdjieff had died. "

"At Prieuré, we drank like hell—vodka, Armagnac. He'd dish it out. All new people got shots—like *that*—but if he suspected you wanted a drink, you wouldn't get anything."

"We had three or four psychological lessons there at the table. He threw out a question: He said, 'Now *Beelzebub* is getting finished, and the Institute is more or less closing, so, what shall I do with my life?' Just like that! And started it from old papasha. We always had a papasha sit beside him. And Olga's de Hartman father was the papasha for years. And he'd mumble the Russian toasts in Russian. And somebody would translate it into French or English. And we'd all drink. Then this question came out: 'What shall I do with my life?' Well, it all went around. It made the rounds from the beginning, and everyone said, 'Oh you have to take ...'—they became clever—'a three year rest ... a seven year rest.' 'You've done so much and you must be very, very tired.' All kinds of Pollyanna things. It's a wonder he wasn't disgusted. After all he had told them and all he had written, everybody felt just ordinarily."

"I knew his brother and they looked alike, but oh, boy! that man was so vacant of anything—he was like an opaque wall. He was named Dmitri. I had more fights with Dmitri .... He's the man who used to steal all the valuable rugs and sell them. You have no idea what effort it was to bring these rugs from the Near East at that time, with the Russian revolution going on. I'd have to go down and buy them back for little or nothing with what little money I had."

"But that wasn't the goal. When I explained the situation to Mr. Gurdjieff, I said, 'It's your brother, he's stealing the rugs out of the study house.' And you know what he used to say to me? 'You shoot him.' Like that. And when I think back, many people alive today would shoot him. 'The Old Man said so.'"

I said, 'No, *you* shoot him, he's your brother. He's your brother, and you shoot him.'

'Well,' he said, 'get the rugs back.'

I said, 'I haven't got any money to get them back.'

'Well, you get it.' And I would get it and buy the rugs back ... to what end, God only knows. Only the effort of putting me on the spot to get the money. Talk about being broke! I was broke all the time. I had nothing!"

Were you in charge of Prieuré at the end?

"At the end I was the only one there. A fifty-eight room house and Rex, the colored boy, whom Mr. Gurdjieff brought over. I didn't have a penny. I was in charge of the gate, and then I was in charge of the whole goddamn place. It was a fifty-eight room chateau, on fifty acres! Walled in."

"That's why Mme. de Salzmann asked me, 'Frankly, tell me honestly, were you the last one at Prieuré?' Yes, I was the last one. I had everything in my possession: All the manuscripts, all the paintings of de Salzmann, all of the music—every goddamn thing. I tried to borrow five hundred dollars. They didn't know what five hundred dollars was. This was during the Depression, around 1932; I couldn't borrow five cents from anybody."

"And then I left. I was the last one there. I closed it as much as closing the gate. And then, Mr. Gurdjieff gave me a party in Paris. And I invited…I didn't know who to invite, because everybody was living in London. There was Tom Peters, brother of Fritz Peters, who was a decent person. And Tom—he came. There was Nick Putnam, who was a descendent of General Israel Putnam; he owned the Putnam stores, which were worth a fortune."

And Mr. Gurdjieff gave you the party?
"He gave me a party in Paris. First he wouldn't listen to me for a couple of weeks. I said, 'I have to leave. I had my sister sell my insurance.' I never had any insurance, but I sold whatever I had to get home. I couldn't work my way home…you can't work your way back. You can work your way here but not back, because so many people jump ship in New York."

"So I decided the best thing to do was just to buy a steamship ticket. It wasn't much. I had a hell of a good time on the trip. I wanted to go on a German ship. I had never been on a German ship, so I went on the *Hamburg*. This was the time Hitler was beginning to raise hell, so there were big racks of Nazi literature all over the place. In the third class dining room you could see the waiters and cooks all lined up, with lots of food on both sides, and then suddenly someone would raise his hand and strike up the band, and it was *Deutchland uber alles,* and they'd come marching out like that with all the food. I'll never forget. I was fascinated by the food—tons of food. But they were all militarized, the whole ship was militarized. I haven't been on a German ship since."

What was the party that was given for you?
"I invited an American girl I knew, Mary Shipman, whose father was the Bishop of Washington (in the Northwest). She had married a French artist, and she had written to me, and I never answered. So finally I wrote to her, 'Will you come to this little party?' There were about a dozen people. These are the people I can remember."

"Mr. Gurdjieff was giving me a champagne party. Nick Putnam walked in, and Mr. Gurdjieff sent him out for a loaf of French bread. Nick came back with a whole armful like cordwood. I said, 'Nick, who the hell is going to eat all that stuff?' This is how crazy Nick was. And then the Old Man spoke. We all drank Armagnac until we were green in the face. It was a wonderful dinner, like no one had ever experienced. Then he spoke about the people, all the bullshit that goes on. He'd make up stories such as: 'Prieuré will now close because Benson is leaving.' Things like that. Of course there was nothing further from the truth than that. I was no force there; I only opened the door. 'And, of course, when Benson makes a fortune, he will help in many ways.' I said, 'Fear not.' Everybody knew I'd never make a fortune, because my mind was never on that kind of thing."

"When I left, the only person who came to the train was the Old Man. He didn't want me to leave."

Why not?

"Well, I was the only one there he could trust. He said, 'You can't do this to me.' I said, 'What the hell can I do? I have to leave now, and go home.' Do you understand the situation you have to get yourself into to break these terrific happenings? That will take up a phase of your whole existence. It's there, to be placed here and be part of you, though not forever. You take on another aim. But nothing is forever. Not that you forget, but you won't put it as the major happening of your existence. Everything is moving all the time. If it doesn't move it's no good. And I'll always end up with that same thing that has affected me, and that is about tradition."

"Mme. de Salzmann wanted to know all about the last days. Mr. Gurdjieff said to me, 'The time has come to sell the Prieuré and I need the deed to the property.' He explained what it looked like—it was a big paper with stamps and a ribbon on it. He said, 'I believe I have hidden it, but I also believe perhaps someone has found it and taken it. So we will look.' We went to the main doorsill and moved a large flagstone that weighed very many pounds. We used crowbars to see if it was hidden under there. Then we moved the flagstones. 'Perhaps it's under here. Perhaps it's this thing, perhaps it's that,' until we came to a room with wooden panels—big wooden panels, the most beautiful things, and he started in with a hatchet. He broke the whole damned panel out looking for the deed. There was no deed there. For historical reasons, there was a tunnel under the Prieuré and it was sealed up in the basement. That was for Mme. de Maintenon. It was built out of stone, like gothic architecture, and it went from the Prieuré to the Fontainebleau palace, which was miles away. I used to fall into this damn thing once in a while. Mr. Gurdjieff said, 'Perhaps I put it there.' I hammered a hole in the brickwork of the tunnel. Very frightened, I got to an obstruction of some kind. I had to go through this hole and a way into the tunnel, looking for the deed with a flashlight, because it was the only safe place on the property. We never found it. Then he had me send telegrams all around the world to various people who had been at the Prieuré. That was a holocaust, that deed business. I can tell you this story which borders on the ridiculous. I think Mr. Gurdjieff was trying me out."

"You know, to talk of things objectively, at the Prieuré there were many, many objectionable things that happened, and some day I'll tell you the wildest story you've ever heard in your life about a person at the Prieuré. Good spirits are created, and so are evil spirits created. The one curious thing is how Mr. Gurdjieff kept this one person there for many years. Because he knew what a real 'svollich' [bastard] he was. He learned things there that he'd put to evil ways. If he got even a grain of understanding he'd apply it the wrong way, and had power that way. He was a small man and he always carried a heavy stick, to show his importance or whatever. And he was quite smart. He came with Mr. Gurdjieff to this country in the early days, years ago."

How do you mean he could use what he learned for evil?
"Well he used it in the opposite way. He had definite force; he learned languages. He learned Russian there, and French, and I don't know how much German. He knew how to squeeze himself into a situation. And, as for the Germans, he plotted to have them broadcast with this girl. It'd make a movie, that story. I was never going to tell that thing because nobody would believe it. But it is absolutely true. There's the curse that could come from...well it's like the Pope who swears to do only Godly things and then turns out to be a real bastard, like the Borgia were. No qualms at all. He learned a hell of a lot at Prieuré."

"Now, we had bastards in our organization, as well as other people. There isn't anybody who can match the stories I know, because I know too damn much of its very beginning and end. Mme. de Salzmann almost had me swear on a bible to tell the truth—if I was the last one there. I said, 'Yes, when the history of Prieuré is written up, they'll know this, the family knows this. When Michele de Salzmann went to London to see Luba, who was one of Mr. Gurdjieff's nieces, for information regarding papers and photographs, he brought back a picture of Rex and me working in the garden."

"Don't mention this to anyone, because someday, if I get furious enough, I'll tell these stories. These are not the stories you will ever hear again."

"And of course, there was Mansfield. She was the wife of the famous editor—he didn't know anything, which was the curious thing. He didn't come to the Prieuré to live with his wife. And Mr. Gurdjieff had her in the stable, to live above the animals, with everything highly decorated … painted and everything. She was so weak; he put her there to get the atmosphere of animals. And he said, 'If she only knew how to draw that.'"

Did you know Katherine Mansfield?
"No. She was just before my time. She was ephemeral, a person who walks around in a mist like a dream. She was an Ophelia. I named her Ophelia myself. She was that type of person. She came and pleaded with Mr. Gurdjieff, saying, 'I will do anything….' And he did the right thing, putting her with animals, trying to teach her how to get this animal force by being close to all the natural forces. And this sounds crazy, but to me it's absolutely true. This is absolutely so. Christ, what experiences I've had in that field. I don't think there's anyone who can top those stories with any of their personal experiences, because these were real personal experiences that I went through."

"I was in charge of making all the roasts of whole sheep, whole muttons, turkeys, chickens … everything. We rented the bakery oven. Do you know what a bakery oven looks like? It's an oval of brick as big as these two rooms where they fire like hell underneath, and they can bake three or four times from the heat of that. We hired that damned thing, and it was my job to get these animals there, and when they were roasted to get them back and place them on the table whole … whole roasts. The food was fantastic."

"I sat here, at about this angle. It was a big oval table, and everybody had their place. Mr. Gurdjieff sat cross-legged on a chair with one leg under him. His bones were as nimble as a baby's. And he'd yell like hell, 'Get my ....' Of course he wore a fez, because he lived in the Near East. They all wore a fez. He was the major-domo of that table, but a 'papasha,' like the oldest man always sat beside him. The papasha had to read, in Russian, all the 'idiot toasts,' to remind us, and start out with the first toast. Everything was Armagnac brandy, and it wasn't just a little shot. There were twenty-one toasts, and they went through all of them, one for each of the idiots. You know, every person is an idiot of a type. The idea is how you see other people and you more or less classify them, consciously or unconsciously. They're this, that and the other thing."

"They classify you, also. I was the 'compassionate idiot.' First the toasts were in Russian, then in French. 'Blu, blu, blu, blu,' you'd hear. It was old papasha. He'd mumble the wrong words, after tons of Armagnac, every type of idiot. I knew them all; I heard them so much. But there was one called 'zig-zag.' First zig and then zag."

"It was fascinating as hell. First came the bath. All day somebody had to fire the boiler to get the steam up for the bath. It was built underground, a really hellish big boiler like a factory with a smokestack."

In what year was Prieuré closed?
"It was closed around 1933 or 1934. I don't know. It was closed when I left, and they went back and forth a couple of

times; he went back and forth. But I left everything. Mme. de Salzmann had a big talk with me when I was with her family at lunch. 'What happened to the money?' she asked. 'Don't ask me, I wasn't there when it was sold,' I said."

"That place was worth a fortune. It was given to the Dreyfus family by the French Government. He died, and it petered out, and we bought it from them. I never fussed over the money. I never thought of it again because I've seen him give money away like that—he never had common sense with it. So when Mme. de Salzmann asked me, 'What happened to the money?' I said, 'God knows…you were with him, you should know.' She was in Paris, though she was not with him. No one knew. But just imagine, I had all this material in my hands. I was responsible. Another time I was taking care of his life…just imagine, I had his life in my hands. Those are the important things in one's life, more than all the other things."

"Because that was my life, not somebody else's, nobody could ever tell you these stories but me, no matter who the hell they are. They don't know half of the picture. When it comes to any of the group thinking, they're a hierarchy, they don't know anything—not about this, but about anything. They're all Ouspensky people, and this institutionalizing is very Ouspensky. That's the difficulty. It's not for me. The Old Man called it 'the institute,' but it was no more institutional than flying a kite. You lived and starved and somehow you lived. For a big party I'd stay up for a couple of days cutting wood just for the fireplace, for the dining room, and that was the only warm room in the house. I worked like hell. No one else has subjected themselves in that atmosphere—just complete subjection to his rule and law and doing the best I knew how. The thing that gets under my skin is truly when people become moralistic. We led an amoral life…a *holy,* amoral life. My life at Prieuré was out of this world."

"People are more alive and aroused by some disastrous thing such as the concentration camps. I always think of that—where death doesn't mean a damn thing. It was just around the corner, but if they had received the full brunt of that shock…many, many things are revealed without anybody knowing. That's my theory. That's the only way I have to be aroused in order for something greater to happen. I have to be aroused by a shock."

"One Saturday, Mr. Gurdjieff left the Prieuré with, I think, five people. I only recognized a Russian typist and Dr. Stoernwald, and here they were, off to Vichy. At about eight o'clock that evening I got a call from Vichy. They had been in a terrible automobile accident and were being treated in the hospital. Mr. Gurdjieff was driving and was in the hospital too. How the accident happened does not matter but I gathered it happened as Mr. Gurdjieff avoided hitting a chicken or some animal. At this time the Russians, Mr. Gurdjieff's family, were living in Paradeu and all the Russian women became very hysterical."

"When they came back from Vichy, Mr. Gurdjieff looked like a battlefield, but he brought them all home. We quartered the women who had been on the trip in various rooms. Dr.

Stoernwald had a hole in his ankle; I think that he never recuperated from that hole and that it finally killed him. Anyway, Mr. Gurdjieff chased all the women out and he said to me, 'Benson, you take care of all the people.' He did not want hysterical people around. He ordered a bottle of Vieux Marc for every room; that is the toughest damn liquor in the world. I went from one room to the other. I told Dr. Stoernwald, 'You should go to the hospital'—but he was very stubborn and said, 'Oh no!' In fact, they all should have been in the hospital. I went in and out of each room all the time."

"You know these metal clips they used instead of stitches? Well, Mr. Gurdjieff sat on the bed, completely undressed. 'Take all these clips off,' he said to me. I said, 'I have no experience, and I have no tools.' 'Make tools. Get tools, get these things out.' I got a pair of pliers and a screw-driver and I boiled them to sterilize them. But I told him that if he started to bleed I would have to get him to the hospital right away. This was at eleven o'clock on Saturday evening!"

"I tore up sheets and made tourniquets. Mr. Gurdjieff looked awful, and we sat there and drank Vieux Marc. I had sense enough to know that you can only keep tourniquets on for fifty minutes and then you ease them off slowly. Mr. Gurdjieff did not say a word—he just drank. It was absolute torture. I got masses of clips out of him. The thing was that when I started slowly easing and taking the tourniquets off, he did not bleed! He just sat there and finally I got him to bed. I went outside and sat outside of his door looking in now and then. He was asleep. I felt he knew what he was doing."

"On my way down to my gate house, I looked every one over in the various rooms. I took some Marc with me and threw myself down. I guess I had slept one hour when I heard the gate click. And there he was, completely dressed, hobbling with a walking stick. I rushed out and said, 'At least wait for me.' I called a taxi at seven o'clock on Sunday morning in France! At least I had him sitting and waiting for me—he was going to walk up the hill to Fontainebleau. As we sat, waiting for the cab, Mr. Gurdjieff said, 'Benson, I'll tell you something, my aim is to finish *Beelzebub,* and not even death will stop me.'"

"We got to the low dive Henri IV dance hall in Fontainebleau, and I gave the taxi driver money to stay right there and wait for us—God knows we didn't have money. The place was open but nobody was in there. It was full of cigarette smoke and the atmosphere of a whirl-a-gig dance hall after a whole Saturday night. I sat him down. Mr. Gurdjieff said, 'Make coffee.' I looked around, made coffee and sat in a corner, wondering what he was writing. He was working on the 'My Father' chapter. It didn't matter if we were in a house of prostitution—wherever life was, that's where he wanted to be, because he absorbed these waste emotions, this wasted life energy, for his own strength. After an hour or so, he said, 'We go home.'"

"I got him to bed. He said. 'Take care of everyone,'—and I did. Mr. Gurdjieff slept. He had done his job—he could sleep now. Dr. Stoernwald was the worst hurt. For the others it was not so bad. Mr. Gurdjieff healed faster than all the rest put together—and I wondered about that. Believe me, these were days I shall never forget. I finally got Dr. Stoernwald to Paris but I think he was never completely right after that."

How long did it take Mr. Gurdjieff to write Beelzebub?
"Through writing and correcting I think it took him...oh, damn near ten years. Almost. Not quite...probably six or seven years. Then he had it all the time. He was correcting it until 1949. In '48 he saw parts of it printed. But he never saw the book. They'd come fifteen, twenty pages in a section. He never saw the book as a book."

12 | *THE ICE HOUSE*

"And she roared … Mme. de Salzmann just roared."

"I'M VERY, VERY HAPPY over at the ice house. It looks as though a tornado struck it, but that doesn't bother me so long as I can hold this line of thought. In the end I really don't care who comes down because I can deal with them. I'll throw them out. But that is the message I wanted to tell you tonight."

"It isn't memory, it's recalling incidents that are indelibly impressed on your mind. Or you can be shocked emotionally, and suddenly you can recall incidents that happened many years ago, even when you were a child. Now, this is the way, in some strange norm, or pattern, or line of endeavor toward understanding, toward more knowledge, I got this. I got this pattern. And that is the pattern of these last few years. You're delving all the time, but that's the pattern I decided to work on. Me! I decided! No amount of conversation with Mme. de Salzmann or anything. The Old Man was dead. And I always tell her, 'I believed in Mr. Gurdjieff. He made impressions on me and, I *know* this is one of the ways! This is one of the ways I work. Especially when I'm at that ice house.'"

"You see, I began at the beginning, at the ice house, when the thing was dilapidated and collapsing, using my wits as to how to straighten it up and keep it in the air. You do one thing after the other, and you grow with that. The building grows and becomes straight and clear, and as it evolves, you don't know it, but that's the way you want it to evolve. And there's not a fancy line on it, except the one innovation on it, which was spearing the building with that tree. I used to tell Mme de Salzmann, 'That's the Nigerian—we're spearing its jaw.' You know how they put a stick right through there? Well, they were all shocked, especially the French were. God, I never saw people get shocked at things like this. You know, that I apply it to humans… For me, that was the best answer I could give to this thing, instead of all the things of strengthening the building. The hell with that. So, that is what I work towards so much—this is what I work towards, whether in battle or whatever."

"The thing that happens is that one, more or less in a hazy way, dwells on something that has happened, like this little conversation, until, after a few minutes that haze is cast off. And it can't be like that [snaps fingers]. That's why I wanted to say I'm glad you went down to the ice house at Armonk in order to look it over, because I'm going to do all kinds of things there. Mme. de Salzmann calls it 'the magicians' workshop,' because we're going to do magic in that place if it kills me. We'll make something odd; we *have* made some odd things. When I was in France this spring, she said, 'Now, you talk.' All these French people were sitting where you're sitting...'Tell them about the ice house,' she said. I said, "Well, they wouldn't understand that.' 'Oh yes,' she said. So I said, 'The ice house is the most beautiful building you have ever seen.' And she roared...Mme. de S. just roared. And she said, 'Wait until you see it.' And I said, 'Well, I think it's beautiful, anyhow.'"

"That's the kind of attachment one gets to what one is doing. It's not a question of beauty. I never wanted that place finished *or* beautiful...always remember that. As soon as we conquer an object, or a project that we're doing, we'll never elaborate on it. I'll cut it like *that*, and we'll start a new one, something else. The gesture has been made. You've gotten all the emotion out of it, so it's finished. You can admire it all you like of course. You keep the objects, but never certain things."

"I have some long range possibilities for what to do. Now, the only reason I'm mentioning this is it's the way I approach a subject. It's not just like that. It's off here someplace, way off; and slowly, slowly, slowly it will come into focus, and we'll do it."

13 | *TIME*

"…cyclical time. I'll use that term all the time until I understand it. I'll get every vibration out of that damned term. 'Cause, you know it'll ring a bell and suddenly I'll understand it."

"FIND OUT ABOUT THIS OTHER TIME. It doesn't need to be named *cyclical*. It can be named another thing in your mind. What, in your mind, *is* time? You may find an answer to why you are alive."

"By this time we should be growing enough to evolve our own tradition. We can't evolve a whole earth. We can't do this, that and the other thing, but we can evolve our own tradition through our own understanding of this thing of being. It doesn't mean everybody should know everything at one time. The Western world thinks they know everything. They know something, but they know *nothing*. All I wanted to talk to you about tonight: find out what cyclical time might be—like that. Historical time is the Western time, European Western time. And here, three quarters or seven eighths of the world do not live within that time. They do not understand. Now, I've said a lot of words. You may think them right, wrong or indifferent.

But you study, study like hell! And read like hell to fulfill your existence, your life, with a kind of understanding what the hell this whole existence is about. Here I am, living tissue. Does this make sense at all? And surely find out about this other time. It doesn't need to be named cyclical…in your mind it can be named another thing. What in your mind is time? You may find an answer to why you are alive. You know, it is a big accident if we are alive. There are ten billion 'germs.' Any one could be picked out…but suddenly you are picked out, you are born. Just imagine…you are born. This is not a plan. This was not a hope for you. But, here I am. Suddenly, here we are. We have been born. But God, I've lived long enough to know that this is not time. That is not the time we're looking for. You know, in a curious way, I don't know what state this is."

"And when it comes to time, time doesn't mean a god-damned thing because time, as they say, is fleeting. Well time, if you go by the clock, suddenly it's twelve o'clock or one o'clock and you have to stop, and here I could go on the whole day without that kind of time. (You know that the expression and understanding of time is so wacky. But I think that if a person could understand time it really means his life, his cycle of life.) That's time; you have completed a cycle. In the meantime you live. From the time you're born you live…and you die. That's when you're supposed to be born and that's when you're supposed to die."

"But the work, our work, is so vast that there are many facets to it. It's on a vast, vast scale. And this idea; I recognize it. I had never solved it any way, because I couldn't solve it, I didn't know enough. I'm beginning to solve that and have a feeling for a greater scope of time than just the ordinary time that I live in. That hasn't much to do with you all, but you will find that out if you do a great research within yourself. Your time that you live today is not the time that we're talking about! It doesn't fit ordinary time. Ordinary conversation doesn't fit the work. The ordinary sense doesn't fit. It has to be done on an extraordinary basis, like that, and almost immediately it will show you where you are in your knowledge and your understanding."

Dr. Philips: "When you say something that you didn't know, you know, yet you feel that it's true. What do you say? Does your conscience ever prick you that you are being a fraud? Or are you able to take it as coming from somewhere?"

Mr. Benson: "No, I don't feel as if it's a fraud. I feel that it isn't strong enough. And through lack of real knowledge it may be right, but it's not strong enough. But it's not fraudulent. There is a terrific question with me always. It's such an accident that, say you, as nothingness was chosen to he born. But think of the millions and billions of eggs that are dispensed with. Suddenly there is one! That amazes me a little bit because I don't allow things like that to get in on me, because I probably shake you a little too much about the question about being born."

Mrs. Benson: "Do you connect that with dying ... that billions and billions don't get anywhere, only some do?"

Mr. Benson: "Yes I think it's by chance, but by chance also millions and billions are not chosen as it were, again because,

I think, like people commit suicide, it happened before and it's easier each time, as they're born it's with them. And they can kill, then, what is known as the soul. It's short circuiting a little too fast, a little too much. Say in, as they say, cyclical time. I'll use that term all the time until I understand it. I'll get every vibration out of that damned term. 'Cause, you know it'll ring a bell and suddenly I'll understand it. But I don't think it happens."

"Everybody has their ideas and I'm telling you some of mine, that I've pondered. You have to reach a central point. And to me, this doesn't have to be proven. I've proved it to myself, for myself. People can believe what I say or not believe it. I'll prove it in many, many ways. And it's not ordinary. But this thing of mankind and ancient civilizations most likely has happened time and time again. To my way of thinking the greatest disaster that mankind has reached is atomic energy. They made atomic energy into the atomic bomb, to start killing thousands of people. The first thing that ever was done with the damn thing was to kill. And that's where we are, you know. Then we start to build up this great, not the war machine, but this atomic thing and other countries have it; and now man *can* destroy himself. It isn't only a fear; it's an actuality. Any one of our pilots can just go and drop the bomb out of hatred or bitterness. Look at the terrific thing we're living through. We're living through a hellish life. And not just locally; it is international. It'll be like fate when this country falls, because there's hardly a country in existence that hasn't fallen. And this is still virgin soil compared with the rest of this civilization. Every country under the sun has fallen, except this country. God knows it won't happen for a long, long time. But it could happen, internally, by sheer accident of forces and the stupidity of mankind, inviting wars and shooting off everything until there's probably nothing left standing, or only a few who live in mountain caves. This country, as a country, has not had an expression of that, of defeat."

"So it exists until there's such a mess that people will have to, somehow, get together. Not to make war materials, but to make ordinary food in order to live. I think the wars are coming to kind of an approach…to a kind of end. I don't think in the course of time that they will exist, because they know goddamn well that they are nonsensical. And I think that probably, within a couple of hundred years, that we'll be approaching this curious thing…. It won't happen overnight, but I think the revolutions are within each country. And revolutions are bloody. Revolutions are not easy things; they will reduce populations all over the world. The large war could come at any moment. But I do think we're going to have more wars and revolutions in almost every country. They'll be within the country, confined within the country."

"The whole system of money as a value has to change. There cannot be only money. It has to be something of value. And, there's no more value, but everything is just, 'How much does it cost? How much will we get?' And it doesn't matter what the hell it is, it doesn't matter what anything is. It's all on money! And that is the big issue that will have to change on this earth. There's not that much money in the universe; what is owed in credit? There's not that much money existing. You think the value of real estate is something. It is nothing. The Indians had it right. There has to be another value to go toward, and not money. Because it's gotten worse and worse…. Look at the strikes; for money and money and money. The cost of living has never gone down—it's always going up. Everybody wants more and more money, thinking that that is security. I think about sixteen percent of our taxes go to the upkeep of the military. Well, that's a hell of a big percentage to protect what? What the hell are we protecting? So, I'll ask the final question. Where are you in life? Not what are you seeking in life but where are you in your understanding of being living tissue in life. And, someone, three hundred years from now at a gathering like this will ask the same goddamn question. It goes on and on until there is a greater, much greater understanding."

"And here we are, facing today. Well, today is a very curious thing to face. It is not conflict between one nation and another. It is conflict within the nation itself. It isn't a question of war between one state and another state. If you can come to a kind of polarity, a nucleus, a line not of how this happened but where the hell is the living tissue going?"

14 | *C L O V E N   H O O F   F A R M*

"It all went up in smoke. So I said, 'The hell with it—
Why do we want to own anything?' The gesture was made.
Why own anything again?"

"I RAISED GOATS, TOO. And you had to fence them in. They could go over an eight-foot fence. Oh, they're clever as hell, goats are. When we bought the farm I told Mr. Gurdjieff, 'Well, we're going to raise goats,' and he thought it was wonderful because he was raised on a sheep and goat diet. And when he came back he said, 'Have you still got the goats?' And I said, 'No.' I said, 'I've only got three.' I didn't make a big farm of it because the cost of fencing was so great, and the depression was still on. He was disappointed. As soon as he walked down the gangplank, he asked me, 'You got the goats?' He wanted goats. And I had this sign I made—it must be in the attic. I carved it—a triangular sign that had a goat's head that I carved on it. I carved beautiful lettering that I copied from a book. A beautiful sign, called Cloven Hoof Farm. And he said, 'What is cloven hoof?' He said, 'You'll never sell any milk, everybody will think of the devil.'

"Cloven Hoof Farm—that's what I named it. My wife thought it was wonderful. Nobody wants to name a thing like that. 'Cloven Hoof' is devilish or Pannish or whatever."

"I studied woodcarving. I had a piece…it must be up in the attic, that sign…I can't imagine where the hell it is. You see, the farm burned down. The chimney always remained. The curious thing I discovered…in all places that burn, the chimney's the only thing that never burns. So the Dutch oven was beside the thing, and I bought this second hand, this door we always had. I painted it nicely, and I used that for important papers—put them in the Dutch oven because in case of fire that wouldn't burn. That's true, and it's a damn good thing. People don't realize that you should make it right in the chimney. You're safe there."

"I felt terrible about that fire. And then I didn't want to own anything. The ownership of things, material things…it's too much responsibility. You're responsible for every goddamn thing you own. And I didn't want to feel responsible. I knew then, for some reason or other, it would stop you in your work, stop you in your tracks if you own tons of stuff. And that's why I didn't care when we bought this place (the house in Mt Kisco). I told my wife, 'I won't look anymore. We buy that or we won't buy anything.' And when she asked about the house, I said, 'I never went into the house…. We can always build a house.' I didn't even want to own a house. You couldn't build the property, but you could build a house."

"Oh, that fire was terrible, you know. We had marvelous things that all went up in smoke—books and paintings, and all the Nonesuch editions. We had some marvelous things. And we used to go up to Vermont or Maine to buy antiques. The most beautiful Shaker stuff you've ever seen. It all went up in smoke. So I said, 'The hell with it —Why do we want to own anything?' The gesture was made. Why own anything again?"

"It was one of the reasons I went to Oregon. Not to start homesteading. The farm burned down about 1943 or '44—somewhere along there. We were out on Long Island, on a weekend, celebrating my wife's birthday, and when we came into the city they told us that the farm was burning. So I said to my wife, 'Let's not go up there tonight.' And of course we were much younger and healthier. So we got Muriel Draper and she drove up with us the next morning. We stopped on the Bronx River Parkway at the Leighton's and had luncheon and about four old-fashioneds, knowing we'd lost the works."

"We got there, and there were just a mass of people, wealthy people we knew in town, with babes in arms and everything, raking over the coals to see what they could find. They came out to see the fire and then they started. These were people we knew in Washington—these people could buy us out at any time. And in a curious way, they saw us just standing there watching this."

"It was like the scavengers who go over a battlefield. You know, like the battle of Waterloo, with camp followers going over the battlefield after the battle. They had to shoot them all. Somebody shot a hell of a lot of them."

"Finally, I went down and said, 'You know, I happen to own this place.' 'Oh, we're just seeing what we can find.' They kept on, and I finally had to chase them."

"Now that is what happens. You can think how awful people can be who want to shoot an animal or shoot a man or shoot something. It's the same with fire. You have a fire, and people rake over the coals … no matter what it is, they'll take it."

"We gave Sandy Calder the piano that my wife's father gave to her, and the beds. They were just scorched; they were all good. We gave him a hell of a lot of stuff. And then I went to Oregon. What the hell, give it all away—I don't want it. It was a hell of a situation."

15 | STORIES

"...and her father said, 'Are you the Rabbi?' I said, 'No, but I'm a holy man.' And that knocked him for a loop."

" I HAD A CHICKEN WHO RAISED PIGS. I called her Victoria. I got a trough, and the whole gang of them ate out of the trough, chicken and all. She'd spend her days chasing the flies from the little pigs, you know. Then finally I would leave the barn door open, and she'd take them out for a walk, all over the barnyard. But if they were frightened by a truck passing by or something they'd race towards her and knock her for a loop trying to get under her—you never saw anything like it. Then she'd take them for a long walk down the road, and they'd follow, come right with her, all the time—she was in charge of them all right. To cool off they'd stay under the bushes right beside the road, and I'd go down looking for them, because I didn't know what the hell she was up to, and not a sound. Evidently she'd taught them chicken language, and they just stayed there if I was yelling, and I knew they were under some bush down near the road. I wouldn't say anything after a while, and I walked back, and they sensed that, and suddenly there she was walking the whole tribe back."

"It was simply wonderful, and I had so many pictures taken of Victoria. The pigs got big, and I kept them all up in a pig run near the children's house, and finally they got so big, they were knocking her all over the place to get at the food, and she had to fight and I thought I ought to retire her, and not let her be killed. She wouldn't have been killed. But she would sit on them, even when they were all together in the run, in the house. She was safe as hell, and I was the one who was stupid."

"I took her away. I put her in the furnace room of the children's house, and that very first night a raccoon got in there and killed her. She would have been safe with the pigs. And that almost killed me, after that whole expression. I broke a whole thing up. I'd never do that again, not under the same circumstances, or under any circumstances. You can't do that kind of thing. That taught me one hell of a lesson, with any kind of animal: I'd never take a mother away. Let them stay forever."

"The reason I got the idea of a chicken was that I had read an article or seen a picture of transporting miniature elephants, little tiny elephants from certain islands in Malay. They send them to zoos all over the world, and they get a bantam chicken—the place is full of fighting bantam chickens—and they set him on the elephant's neck. He sits there as a companion all during the trip, and the elephant doesn't get upset because he has animal contact. So I got the idea of the chicken."

"Now, I have that kind of understanding, and that is what I wish to express: something better, and better, and better. Not for the pigs and not for the chickens, but because there's a better kind of existence in that story and we could really come to it."

"Most of the pigs that I raised I raised at Mendham. But I had pigs up in Maine, and I had the pig killer come, and I thought he would tie them down like they do in France. Instead, it was in the snow. And he just stuck them and they walked all over. It looked like a battlefield, and I was so goddamn furious. And then he took them to town. He was to butcher them and clean them. He got half a pig for killing the two pigs—that was his pay."

"Years ago in Maine, people were poor. They didn't have the money for hiring help. They bartered. It was a real barter system. And I'll never forget the time I had this dead pig... my God, they stretched to about seven or eight feet... in the hallway. My mother was so damned furious. I said, 'He has to cool and be aged.' I wasn't frightened, but she was frightened to death of this dead pig in the hall."

"Then I had to make a big oak barrel. I had a formula I got from Birdseye for how to pickle pork, and I lost the damn thing. Six weeks in brine, saltpeter, all kinds of mixtures to measure—I made this brine and cut the hams, the bacon, the head; everything went into this barrel and soaked for six weeks. And the soaking—it has to go right to the bone. If it doesn't it will rot inside. I made sure it went right to the bone. Beautiful hams, my God!"

"And then out of a big drum, a barrel, I drilled holes to hang broomsticks on. I hung the hams and the bacons, and I made a smoke house out of a big barrel on the stones with a stovepipe some fifteen or twenty feet away in the snow to keep the pipe cool. I had a fireplace outside with hickory smoke and that went up the flue and out. You take a gauze or mesh or something, and you don't close it entirely, but let it draw. And, boy! I had the most beautiful smoking oven. It was as dark as this. By that method—I discovered the method myself—I built the whole damn thing. And it really smoked those things. Well, it took days, probably a couple of weeks. I was at it all the time. It was in the late winter or early spring."

"I had dogs. There was no trouble with animals. We never had any animals come down on account of the dogs. And I tell you, I had hams—my God, they were the best hams I ever had in my life. That was living, a real, wonderful living, everything fresh all the time. But that's where I learned about pigs. And when I went to France, I knew about pigs. They kept the pig for two years until he weighed almost a thousand pounds. Big, big, pigs—you never keep them that long in this country. I used to raise all the pigs in Mendham. About forty-five I'd ship, according to their size."

"Pigs are wonderful. People should know about pigs. They're the most intelligent of all the animals. Everybody says they're dirty, 'like pigs in a pig sty.' They're not dirty. They're the cleanest of all the animals. I had them running in a big orchard in Mendham. I had a pig trough that I had to anchor. They'd root it up, like that. But pigs always make a section, like the Ethiopians, for their toilet, and never where they are lying down or eating—never!"

"There was a French peasant in the valley of the Rhone. Where there is great water, there can always be great desert. Nothing grows on the banks of the Euphrates River; the river flows on, but it's absolutely dead. The land in the Rhone valley slowly became desert. All the people in the hamlets began to move out. But this one peasant refused to move. He went around the various forests, and he walked miles and miles to collect seeds, such as acorns and beechnuts and things like that, and he started planting them deep down in this dry sand. And suddenly, these trees came up, in a great perimeter of twenty miles. The French forestry service came over and said, 'How wonderful … it's all coming back.' It took ten years for them to find out what the hell happened."

"Victor Hugo was locked in Notre Dame tower, and I was also. I stayed all night in Notre Dame tower overlooking Paris, and I didn't give a damn. I slept down in the church. In the morning, out of a wall came a monk. I don't know where he came from, but he came out of a wall, to light candles. He let me out, and that was that."

I love the story about the French peasant that was paralyzed. "Oh, that's not my story, that's Zola's. Emile Zola told a story of a French peasant family, a man and his wife, who had a small hotel, and they worked like hell. The French can work like the very devil. He had a stroke and became paralyzed, and his wife had to do all the work in the place alone. She thought, well, you know, by God he's *alive*... he should be able to do something. At least *one* thing. And she thought it all over, and then, you know what she did? He was stretched out, and she placed eggs all around him, and she had him hatch chickens. Isn't that a wonderful story?"

"I was sent to inspect a ship once, and I had to put oilskins on, from head to foot. It was between the ship's outside wall and the inside wall, where the bilges were, way down on the bottom. You had to curve your body in... you just fit yourself in this thing and trail an electric lamp. The ship was floating; it wasn't in the dry dock. I was a goddamn fool, and had no fears, and I squeezed my way along, then the light short circuited and went out, and some ship or something passed that made the ship roll, and the goddamned bilge water came right up to my neck. Then I got frightened, and when you're frightened you swell, can't move anywhere. Everybody says, 'He's so frightened he can't move.' It isn't that—you just can't move physically. I was way the hell in there, without a cord or a signal or anything."

And the water was up to here?
"Well, when she tipped, when she rocked back and forth. That was from a passing ship. And it was awful stuff, whale oil and what the hell, but I had to go in there. There was a

valve that wasn't functioning. I think it was just frozen. They had never tried it, and they wanted to see if they couldn't pump the bilge. I'll tell you now, I was sent in because I had no fear of that kind of thing. But I never figured on the damn boat rocking."

Was that during World War II?
"No, that was right after the first World War when I was around New York, just doing this, that and the other thing. They asked me to go in there, and I said sure, I'd go in there. Nobody wanted to do that. But we had a friend, a crazy fisherman, named Little Collie, and we called him Lilla Collie. He was a Newfoundland banks cod fisherman. He probably was a great fisherman. Collie was always in difficulty. And he took a job…. It was 1908, when they dug the Hudson tubes, and oh, Christ! men were killed right and left in those things."

"They had to go into these banks. It took two and three-quarter hours to get on the job by going through the stages of pumping compressed air. Sixteen pounds. By the time you got there, you were worn out. I had never been through one of those things. They had the compressed air going through the mud of the Hudson river. The compressed air held up the mud banks as they were digging, then they'd add another sleeve."

"Evidently they struck a weak spot in the mud of the river, and a big rush of air blew out a hole right at the end of the casing, which just went right out, and Little Collie went with it. He went through about fifty feet of mud in the compressed air—it pushed him right out. Now, you wouldn't believe that, but this guy went through the Hudson River and out, and he lived, that was the thing."

And you knew him?
"Oh, I knew him very well. He just took a job there. We read about a man being pushed right through the goddamned river, the mud and water. It was a geyser, I guess, that shot up. But I never forgot that damn story. Lilla Collie. Queer eel. And then he went to see if he could do better down in Louisiana. He got on the train, and he didn't have any money. He had a ticket in his hat, and he just posed at the open window, and when the conductor shook him, he shook his hat off and there was a ticket in it. It wasn't a real ticket. He got a trip all the way home for free."

Oh, it was deliberate?
"Oh, yes. He had it all planned. Lilla Collie always had some wacky, wacky thing; not evil, you know. He needed the ticket. He got on the train, the conductor shook him, and his hat went overboard…. These are the people I liked. I never laughed so much in my life at some of the wacky experiences."

"I had two experiences in Maine where I had absolutely no fear. Portsmouth Navy Yard was five miles away, and a sailor had come up with the tide. He drifted in a boat, and he landed on our beach, up the river. He broke into one of the houses that a woman happened to be in, and she locked herself in a bathroom and started yelling. I was across the road, and I heard her, and I just fell out of the bed right outside the window. I went over there, and I put on the lights, and there was this sailor—United States Navy. He was a little crazy. 'Oh,' he said, 'I wasn't doing anything.'"

"And I said, 'What are you doing here, anyhow?' And I took him into our house, and then I said, 'Well, here's a cot, in my room.' My mother was there. She wasn't afraid of anything. I gave him a little bite to eat, then I looked over his clothes and everything. He had come from Boston, but he really was a little crazy. I called up the Navy Yard for two days, but they wouldn't send an ambulance or a patrol or anything whatsoever. I had to take him to the Navy Yard. I pushed him into the gate and told a marine guard to hold him there and not to allow him out. Then the navy heard about it and they sent two secret servicemen, 'What was I making such a fuss about?' I said, 'You have a crazy man in the navy. And you dare allow him to go out like this? And I've been yelling for a week.' Oh, I was furious at those bastards."

"In the fall of the year, when I had all the animals in the barn, I worked like hell. I put boards up and then filled the cracks with manure so there wouldn't be any draft, and with the first snows, I'd throw snow over them. One night—it was about a hundred yards from where my house was—I heard the pigs and the animals, and I looked out. There was no light, because they slept, and there were noises all night."

"So I went down there. I went into the barn, lit the light, and there was a real idiot in among the pigs, just staring—a real idiot. I said, 'Well, what are you doing?' He couldn't talk. The pigs were tame, thank God, or they'd have killed him. I got him out. I said, 'You live this way?' and he said, 'Yes.' So we walked about a half-mile. It was a drizzly end of October day, and so cold that there was almost ice, and he walked right in back of me, step by step. I wasn't frightened, I can tell you that; I wasn't frightened at all."

"We had gone far enough, and we turned around and came back, and I said, 'Do you live that way?' There was a place called Kennard's Corners where a street car would come by—they had coastal street cars then—and I turned around there and he walked right in back of me. I took him into the house, and my mother said, 'Oh, the poor boy!' and felt sorry for him. We searched his pockets, and he had a grocery list. He wasn't unkempt at all, clean and everything. But wouldn't you think someone would sew a name and address onto him?"

"This was about eleven o'clock at night. We had a big pot of stew that night, and he ate most of it. Then I put him in my room, on a cot, and kept him there for a week. I asked everybody did they know him? He would come with me. I didn't dare leave him alone because if he got in the barn, if he had matches, even he could set that whole place on fire, and that barn had an awful lot of cattle and horses and goats. Anyhow, he stayed with us there. It was the time of getting apples in, and I was working like hell, and he'd follow me around like a little dog. I was never afraid except if he was out of my sight."

"Well, anyhow, the local butcher came by—he was a traveling butcher. He said, 'Oh, yes I know them...they live in Eliot, and it's a way down this way. And they're the wealthiest family in the town.' He told me the name, and said, 'I'll be driving by.' I said, 'No, I'll call them up.'"

"So I called them up, and they came right away. They'd been looking for him. They even called the police, and they never, never got over the idea that my mother and I took care of him without calling the police, because if we'd called the police, they would have put him in jail. And idiots, at that time, were allowed to be kept by their family. They came in a big Cadillac and they never stopped thanking us and asking what did they owe me? I said, 'You don't owe us anything.' And on Christmas, my God! what a load of stuff they gave us! Every damn thing you can imagine, for this gesture. They never got over the idea that I didn't call the police to get rid of him. They'd stop by all the time. Well, that kind of understanding and good will, without fear of any kind, that registered. He'd have stayed forever, because he didn't know where he was."

"I wanted to tell you those curious things about crazy people. I'm never afraid of them; I know my mother wasn't. Oh, no, we have to keep him. She wasn't afraid of anything. But as we go through life, we gather more fears about crazy persons. Now I have more fears than I had then."

"You know, I know in a curious way, what I think half the night through, and at times I wonder, what the hell am I doing? Am I crazy, insane? What's wrong with me? No one says anything that I can even recognize. So I wonder about myself. Where is this creature going? And I often look back, because you have to look back, as you have to look ahead. You have to live your life and look ahead, and I often look back to when I used to do things that were so meaningful. I lived in wonderment."

"I used to go to the Halles market and pay my ten centimes for a bowl of soup that was made in big cauldrons. The butcher and the vegetable people would throw all their wares into these cauldrons, and you'd pay ten centimes for a big bowl of stew, and it was simply out of this world. And then I'd go to St Eustache, an unfinished cathedral, right on the corner and hear the most heavenly voices, the greatest choir in all Paris. This was real for me. All for nothing. You existed. There was no question of having to buy a ticket. That is what I mean by the fallacy of money—it doesn't have to be. Of course, you can say that I should have lived a hundred years ago, in another age, and enjoyed that kind of thing. But I'm living today and I do not believe in this whole money thing. I think it is one of our mistakes in this civilization. What the hell is money? It's all paper. No matter how you look at it, everything is a piece of paper, and the value of this paper is the thing we're living by. So let us recognize it as paper and get along with a kind of a barter system before it cracks this whole civilization wide open through the fallacy of power through money. That's what we're on the brink of right now. It's being expressed right along the line. There are other ways. It's not a question of 'love', but there can be an expression.

There's no joy in this civilization. And probably the earth has witnessed this kind of thing many, many times."

"It's a very curious thing that we are alive, and part of the human race, and evidently thinking that we're going to be here one hell of a long time. And things will carry on as we are doing. But everything changes; attitude changes and, as they come into power, they think that it is always as it is now. And the next generations, three or four hundred years later, think this is it; that is it, like that. There is no answer to that kind of thing. We have to get to what in hell keeps us alive and what life is about. And that may never, never happen. Therefore, the human race will carry on and on through lack of knowledge. The more we get into this scheme of things, say, of technology, or how to do things better and better, the more we are 'licked.' We'll get less and less until they find out that that is not the way of existence. The best story I can think of to illustrate this was about a group of Germans who went into Tibet and found silver mines, gold mines and everything. They had pack animals packing it all out. And they were captured by the Tibetans and they made them bury it back into the earth…every bit of it. That's a part of the earth and should not be disturbed. I think it's a most marvelous story."

"I went to the Epstein house for the circumcision of a child. I was sitting there watching everything, and her mother and father came in from Florida and looked at me, and her father said, 'Are you the Rabbi?' I said, 'No, but I'm a holy man.' And that knocked him for a loop. They didn't know what to make of that."

16 | *T H I N K I N G*

*"So I thought things over and I said, 'You know, you hear
of things, but I've been thinking differently. I think we
are born pure and with being, as a baby, and as we grow
older and civilization crawls in, it's not a question of
do this or do that—this seeps out of us.'"*

"I OFTEN WONDER, 'How do people think?' Now, what my bent
is, thinking things over from day to day, and a kind of making
sense of something, in a greater scope. And then you reduce
it until it comes that the only answer for anything is yourself.
You don't reduce it to a condition. You reduce it to a pinpoint,
yourself. And that is more or less what your belief is, if you
do believe in anything. I often thought there isn't anybody
who can say he is an anarchist or an atheist. They always say,
'I don't believe in anything whatsoever,' until you come to the
point: 'Do you believe that you're alive and do you believe in
yourself?' 'Yes.' Well then I said, 'Then you believe in something.' There's not one who doesn't believe that he's alive. And
he believes in himself. That what he's doing is right. Then he
believes in something. There's no one who's a real atheist.
They have to believe in something. And they do. And then to
get to the point where your belief makes sense, and making

sense, you talk about it here and there, you make nonsense, and you laugh about it. You have to do gymnastics with what you make sense of. Otherwise it'll become so droll and so impossible and so low in thinking and so deadening that you won't be able to live. Your sense of humor is gone. That's why ministers went almost nuts, and minister's families. There's no sense of humor. Only these two things of the…What do they call them? The Albigensians believed in right and wrong, black and white. And that's where they were almost doomed to extinction. They didn't come to a third force. I believe there has to be a third force, a neutralizing force. There has to be something in between. Otherwise it can become so god-awful. Never joke, never…always moralistic. You lose the whole sense of living. And of course, I never did that. I was never a great moralist. I never could make a law…forbid people this, that, and the other thing, because I believed in almost everything that the human mind and emotions and body can do. I just believe in it—like that, and in working toward that end, of a kind of self-development, or self-understanding. Knowing what you're doing almost all the time. I stick strictly to a line, say on weekends, here at the ice house, and I stay within that area of thought and doing and knowing. In a sense, I get the strange feeling that I know more than all of them put together—the ones who are in that little gathering and listening. Sometimes I wonder and I say, 'Don't you ever think of anything at all? Because you never hear anything.' And I swear, people are not thinking and, perhaps, adding and adding and adding to a little bit of knowledge, toward a little bit of understanding, toward a sense of being. Frankly, if I may say so, that's what I'm attempting to do."

"Today I was fighting on the phone with Halstead Quinn [the power company]. Since last Monday, I've been calling them up to come up and clean up the furnace and fix the thing. They kept putting me off. That was Tuesday. I call them up on Wednesday and say, 'Now, when are you coming?' But while I was talking, in all the fury, I was thinking about what I've been telling you, all at the same time. Thinking of this other thing—this seriousness. I wanted to show the fury, like that, because nothing has happened. But while I was going through that, I was thinking of this other thing. That was more on my mind than what I was yelling about. I wanted to go through with that, so I said, 'You call me, I've been calling you the whole week.' And I let it go at that. I don't care what I do in that sense. This other thing means more to me—to have that kind of understanding, not trying to justify something that'll never be justified. This other thing is your life's work, more or less your life inside to think about. People wouldn't even have to know anything about it, and you can be working towards something greater than yourself as you are now. Something you could be. So I hold that sacred."

"I often thought with that line—say, a person like Julius Caesar—is what he thought when he was being killed. What the hell did he think of when he was losing his kingdom? When everything was going, including his life? What does a person think of in that moment? He knows it's going. He must have known for minutes before. And that's the end. That's your time. That's your end."

"So I thought things over and I said, 'You know, you hear of things, but I've been thinking differently. I think we are born pure and with being, as a baby, and as we grow older and civilization crawls in, it's not a question of do this or do that—this seeps out of us. It seeps out of mankind. And when is the moment of stopping that seepage? Maybe never. Maybe we just live through life and die off as if nothing. And here we're preaching to grow in being.'"

"Now, if that means that we have to stop this seepage and return to what has been lost of our purity, of our deep sense of being, then I believe in the form of things that I said. I was born that way, and I have to retrieve that. You don't retrieve it but you stop the seepage."

"That is why I'm such a bastard and a rebel, not wanting to gain more or have this, or have that and everything, and that is where I can make contact with people … because I am that. I have more than they have. Or I have more than a lot of people have, in a sense, in order to make contact. I don't care who it was, and this is one of the great goals. Do you understand that line of thought? It isn't entirely backwards, but it isn't directly on that line. And, of course, everyone's out to kill me on this kind of thing. And this, I said, is your canon law. This is your tradition, and why you react this way. But this is my tradition—I have to put something of myself in this work to make the tradition continue."

"Even in Chartres Cathedral they had the simple tower, the perfectly built tower. Then comes the fifteenth-century tower, with all the curlicues on it. That is mankind to me, a higher order of things. I think of it a great, great deal. And it has to be a dual thing, like the great blue domed mosque. It's so beautiful. But you know what they use it for don't you? The smoke of the incense goes up into the tower and collects as a heavy soot from which they make their ink, because it comes from a holy temple. Isn't that fantastic? That's what they use, because there's no other place to get it. You see, Bennett spent a lot of time in Turkey. He was with the British army in the First World War, as a captain or some damn thing. He spent a lot of time there; he went to all the temples and everything. He said they burn a certain kind of incense, wood smoke or something, and he said it gathers in the dome and they sweep this soot into a pot and that's what they make ink out of. You know I almost died listening to this. And he said that's where they make their ink. I like Bennett, you know, because he was full of these tales. He listened, he watched, he heard, and he remembered. He remembered many, many things. Bennett had more vision than a hell of a lot of people in our work here have. He does fantastic things and he gets involved and I don't hold anything against him no matter what the hell he does. I think, in a curious way, that this is what I'm talking about, because this kind of ink is not manufactured with all the chemicals in it. It's the purity of the thing that comes through fire and smoke."

"I believe in the thing that we're born this way, and the idea is to stop losing it, to stop the floodgates of achievement of being; of civilization, not mankind but civilization."

"Like that man in the woods, he had more. Because he had so little, he had so much more understanding of the natural forces and what he would have to do in order to live, if he wished to live. If a forest fire came, if the floods came, if water came, and if his house was disintegrated here and there, he'd repair it. But with his littleness, he had a tremendous force."

"There's nothing more pure than a helpless infant child, and the reason is that the child is almost all liquid. Did you know that? There's hardly any solidity. You can twist their bones like knots. And that's why children suffer more than older people in fire. The children suffer and die, not from the smoke but on account of the liquid. They're all liquid—the opposite of the fire. The purity of this earth and not of this earth, all at one time, has to be nurtured. That's my only proof. A newborn baby is my only proof."

"And I love some of this Octavio Paz thing. [*Claude Levi-Strauss: An Introduction,* by Octavio Paz] Maybe this is what I believe in. But what the hell do *you* believe in? Deep down, not bullshit but deep down, what does a person believe in?"

"It just struck the right note. There's a great depth of time that man has to figure on. Then there's historical time, of which there's hardly a thing that I can't talk on or know about. I don't want to know these goddamn things. It's like owning things. I put my forces into that kind of recall, instead of a greater recall. At times I strike upon it, but that was from my early childhood. I have put through stopgaps of different kinds of beliefs, and being able to retain what I have. That's where my measure of development is. Is it development? Paz talks of a void in there. Is that void emptiness or is it full? It's for us to be able to recognize its fullness. You understand the kind of battle that goes on? We think that a void is just empty space. Not necessarily. It can be full, and we haven't got the wherewithal to see it, to recognize and identify and seek."

"There was a minister, years ago, a Presbyterian from Maine who was talking to his family. He was talking about life and death and he said, 'We have lived and are living, but death can be no further...' And he said, 'like that' and dropped dead. This actually happened on a porch in Maine. Well, it was an accident—it just happened. It was no accident."

About Nietzsche
"You know, my thoughts are like that, but I can't write like that. He's the bastard, but in time he will not be the bastard. I don't think he cared what they called him or what he was a part of. He was probably mad...most likely he was mad, but mad to such a degree that he could see. Mad people can see a hell of a lot more than normal people. They can be put away, but they see something wonderful."

"I think Nietzsche was like that. He may have been a real bastard, but oh boy! You know, he was before Freud. Machiavelli was the person for Nietzsche. Nietzsche could never get over *The Prince*. Machiavelli was just so anti-Christian—at a time when you had to be Christian in order to live, or you were burned at the stake. Most likely, Machiavelli was a kind of super mind lost in Satan and the devil instead of the Christian idea of building all these wonderful things when it's not really true. I don't know where Machiavelli drew this material from but I think he drew it from some really great force and produced *The Prince*. And I think Nietzsche's interest was piqued. I may be so absolutely wrong. Nietzsche was considered the devil incarnate. But you have to realize that he was a force against all the nonsense that was going on, and he wasn't accepted. We still fight over these two things: Nietzsche the good holy man and at the same time, Nietzsche the devil. He was against the order of things."

"I think he put himself into a position where he could be thrown into an insane asylum. God knows, we know so little—we know a great deal. I know so little that I hardly have the right to think about this. But, when I think of what I know, I make my own judgment about Nietzsche. He was neither of these people. He's not a holy man, and he's not the devil incarnate. I think all people who know anything are considered crazy."

"You know, I have a habit of thinking all the time. And I have to stop—stop thinking—absolutely. Wacky things, like why did Alexander go into his conquering process, all the way to India? Things like that. It wasn't anything. He was only twenty-six years old. He was the greatest conqueror in the world."

"I think most likely it's my thoughts invading the situation where I don't give a damn. What the hell—who thinks? Not that I say I think. Who is in possession of their faculties? That is my main worry. I wish I was. I want to be, and that's the terrible thing. I'm dying on account of that. It's that I'm not in possession of what is in me. It's not reading, and it's not what one remembers in reading. This is what I go through almost every night. You're a living creature, and why are you seeking to know?"

"I don't want to read about it. The fight has to be the big fight with oneself, through the understanding of what you're thinking about. And through that understanding you may gain knowledge, and there is your attempt. One's only possibility is to pay, at once and in full. And so, now, to go into a sense of being, not the interpretation, makes me better."

*Martin Benson. Read at St. Vartan's Cathedral
on January 15th, 2011*

*[At a time when this book was still in preparation, Roger
Lipsey asked me if something could be read from it at the
January 13th celebration. Taking a paragraph here and a
story there I pieced the following reading together. With a
single exception, the reader will recognize everything in it as
a repetition of what s/he has already read in one or another of
the preceding chapters. The exception is the story of Mr. Gurdjieff's car accident. The far more vivid and detailed account
that appears in chapter 11 only came to the surface after the
reading had already been given. —ED.]*

"There is a massive story that no one dares touch upon, and
that is the real story of Gurdjieff's life. You see, everybody has
a story of Mr. Gurdjieff. But aside from personal impressions,
there is the story of his existence. There are many, many things
we have to agree upon. And that is never mentioned, never.

Oh, boy, talk about blood and thunder. And the women ...."

"No, what I'd like to do is write about this Work. I want to give my expression, and tell how I loved the Old Man and believed in him. But there are a few things that have to be adhered to, and one is that the story has to be honest and truthful, as I am naturally honest and truthful."

"The reason you're in this kind of work is that this has more force than you do. Therefore you will be part of it in order to help you gain more force. Once you have accepted this work, you have taken a part of a force that actually does not belong to you. You have taken a part of God's force. Because this is His job, if you want to know — to pull people together. You have taken a part of this force upon yourself. And forever and ever and ever you are both blessed and cursed. You cannot blame anyone but yourself. And you know of nothing better, because you have struck a core of something that exists, and therefore you work toward that core."

"The only real power is for a person who arrives at an understanding with enough knowledge and background for a sense of being. This sense of being will be felt by everyone. And then you are, more or less, a person who has arrived at something, no matter how small, that could be a force. Outside of that there isn't any force. Appointments are no force. And of course you don't get all your knowledge from one source, because if you only stick to one theme, then it's not only lukewarm, it's warped."

"The one thing that kept the Old Man very straight was memory, and he told me that when he was hurt in that first accident in 1924—he said, 'The one thing...the one thing was that I remembered myself.'"

"He was unconscious for days. Christ, I thought he was dead. They found him across the road with his shoes off beside him. He had taken his shoes off. He was sitting on the opposite curb. The police found him. I think the shock was so great that, probably, not realizing it, he took his shoes off as if he were going into a mosque or a temple, because that was the habitually respectful thing to do. And maybe he was near death, because I know when he came out to have the men cut the trees down, he wasn't talking at all. But he knew how to absorb life. It was necessary to become stronger in order to get life, to become enriched and stronger. He knew how to take this force from live trees."

"And he sat in the wheelchair. We didn't know at the time, but later on I figured it out. I told you that story about the Café de La Paix. He was always sitting there, like Toulouse Lautrec in a brothel. He sat right in the middle with all this life—mostly Americans—and emotions and joviality, and whatever...all wasted emotions. He was writing *Beelzebub*, and I would swear he would steal these emotions because they were going wild and astray. He had that kind of force. That sounds so crazy, but where else could he get his strength from, except the taste of all people? He never mentioned it, but I figured it out from what he said I had to do. He said, 'The waste of emotions, the waste.... Get among crowds of people.' He said, 'The best crowds to be among were the holidays, the holy days, or Christmas. You go to the cathedral and you get yourself into as objective a state as you possibly know, and you steal their prayers.'"

"I used to go to Saint Eustache. They had the most wonderful choir in all France. I sat and listened and tried to get into an objective state in order to take their prayers. And he approved. He said, 'You take their prayers for your development, your welfare, your strength, because they are going to waste. They have not the force or power or understanding to reach their God.' That was the message. He said, 'They could reach their God if they knew how.' Then he told me, 'You have the wish to reach your God. It comes from you, and as you develop you can reach your God. And then you take strength from your God or from that force and take it back to you — It's like this: that's the motion. It has to start from you, though. Begin with the desire, the wish, and then, religiously, you study that in order to reach something higher and greater — in order to bring it back to you.'"

"He could do it because of how when he was hurt so badly, he was taken out in a wheelchair and had the men cut trees down and dig up roots at all hours of the night. He sat there to absorb the life of the trees for his physical welfare. This guy was unconscious. I swear he was dead, for days and days, and he pulled through. Then he used people, the lives of people. He'd get into the middle of the Café de la Paix with all the emotions and everything going to hell while he was writing. He knew how to steal their wasted emotions, which were just going out into the atmosphere. He knew how to recover. He knew what to do."

"People are more alive and aroused by some disastrous thing, such as the concentration camps. I always think of that—where death doesn't mean a damn thing. It was just around the corner, but if they have received the full brunt of that shock…many, many things are revealed without anybody knowing. That's my theory. That's the only way I have to be aroused in order for something greater to happen. I have to be aroused by a shock."

"Mr. Gurdjieff had been in a very bad accident. He was cut all over and the doctors had put clips on his wounds. One Sunday morning, when I was at the gate, he came walking toward me, just crawling along. And told me to remove all the clips. 'My God,' I told him, 'you'll bleed to death.' I was terrified. I had his life in my hands. But he insisted and I removed all of them. Then he told me to drive him to Fontainebleau where there was this terrible low dive of a café he liked to work in."

"He worked at that café on Sunday mornings. I just walked in and opened up the place, and made coffee for him, and it smelled to high heaven. The café was a whirligig dance hall Saturday night, and this was a Sunday morning. The place was wide open, and here we sat. He was finishing the *My Father* chapter. It didn't matter if we were in a house of prostitution—wherever life was, that's where he wanted to be, because he absorbed these waste emotions, this wasted life energy, for his own strength."

"And he said: 'I'll tell you, my aim is to finish *Beelzebub*, and not even death is going to stop me.'"

"I see Mr. Gurdjieff sitting on the moon just watching, looking at the whole universe and this earth. And that's where I put him: looking down on the whole fallacy of mankind, on this earth, and sending various emissaries from various planets to this earth."

"Not that he was holy or anything like that. He had this force. You see, I have a theory: In a curious way, there is a Jesus Christ living at all times, and it's not a person so much as a polarity that has to be. This curious polarity has to be in order to hold this earth together. The form can change, but the force is always there. Always remember that: The force exists. I don't think there has been only one curious Jesus Christ.... In that sense they do exist on the face of the earth, somewhere. You can't prove this kind of thing. But I feel there has to be that kind of thing in existence at all times, and their food is mankind. When mankind passes out, they'll pass out."

"Do you understand the situation you have to get yourself into to break these terrific happenings? That will take on a phase of your whole existence. You take on another aim. Nothing is forever. Everything is moving all the time. And I'll always end up with that same thing that has affected me, and that is about tradition."

"We can live this tradition, but do not split hairs over it instead of developing, using the tradition as a source of surprise, but not as the law. You are the law. You are the judge. There are certain objective basic laws, but you are within yourself. About the tradition I always say this thing that Abelard said: 'Tradition is alive, when it can inspire the creation of new work.' I think that's the most marvelous sentence I've ever heard—not a negative word in it, nothing about what *not* to do. 'Tradition is alive when it can inspire the creation of new work.'"

"There is a photograph taken at our wedding, with Mr. Gurdjieff. I haven't seen it for years. He stands in between us, hanging onto us and laughing like hell. It's the only picture in the world where you see him laughing."

"Did I tell you the story of that wedding? We went up with Muriel Draper to find a little church in Stamford because Orage was married there. And we decided that the Old Man would be there that week, and we invited about fifteen people. As we got ready to walk down the aisle—there was music, the minister was ready—but we couldn't find the Old Man. We didn't know where he had gone. So we had to wait. And suddenly he just walked in. When the minister asked him how he was related to us he said, 'I father both.'"

"After we were married he used to come up there to the place we rented in Woodbury. We had a maid, but he'd chase her out and do all the cooking himself. He loved to cook, but he cooked enough for an army and there were only a couple of us there. We let him do anything. That's when I went to the Russian village with him."

"There was a Tolstoy village near Newtown. I found out they had a printing press, and I asked him if he wanted to go. My wife and I drove him over, and he spoke Russian to them. It was Tolstoy's nephew or something. And he said, 'I think we can have *Beelzebub* published there.' And he almost made a deal. You couldn't control him."

"Then one day he had these *Herald of Coming Good* books that were written while I was at Prieuré. He had them in Russian, English and Spanish, cases of them, with him. I got the Russian cases and put them in the car and the next day we drove up to the Russian village and I took out a mass of them in my arms."

"We had to climb this long hill, in the cold October rain, and we slipped all the way up. He went ahead, and I followed with these books. There was a line of cabins up the hill, and at each cabin he knocked on the door, and said in Russian, 'Will you please read this?' I gave him the books one book at a time, and he gave them away, going from one cabin to the other. I'll never forget that."

"He gave them out himself. His point was, as he said: 'All those who are in the Work have to pay for the printing of *Beelzebub*.' And we did pay, we all paid four hundred dollars. We had to pay for the publishing, and then we gave them away—talk about a new idea! He said, 'We all have to go around with copies and give them to the people on the streets of New York.' I can just see myself on Fifth Avenue and Forty-Second Street saying, 'Will you please read this?' and handing them out. That's the way it was going to be, and we would have done it."

"There's another story, a funny one. We never understood it. Mr. Gurdjieff was on the way to Brighton Beach, on the boat, to see the Whitcombs. They went to pick him up and he said his wallet was stolen and he lost his passport. I'd like to see anybody rob him, because he was aware of everything going on all the time. I said, 'How did it happen?' He said, 'I don't know, but I have to report.' I think he threw the damn thing overboard. I never could understand how anyone could rob him. I think he threw it out, just to see what we would do."

"They put him on Ellis Island, with all these immigrants, and especially Rabbis who came from here and there. And he had a wonderful time. Now, what values do you consider? When I look at the remarkable men, there are a hell of a lot of them I wouldn't say were remarkable at all. To say you had a whale of a time on Ellis Island...."

"I thought when I lived at Prieuré that I was an orphan. I used to ask Mr. Gurdjieff questions and he'd say, 'Oh...' And he'd throw me aside like that. Or, when I insisted, he would come back a week later and say, 'You haven't come to that. No matter what I would say you would never guess it.' So then I stopped and I felt like hell. One day, arguing on the telephone (we argued every day on the telephone, we couldn't understand each other) and I said something, and he said, 'I'm coming right out and we will have coffee.' For no reason at all. Now, what I said, I don't know, but he knew. We went up to his room and had coffee, and he spoke to me for about two and a half hours, answering my question. And here I felt like such a heel, thinking I was forgotten."

"He told me the whole work. He said, 'You were not ready for that particular answer.' It was something vital to me. I don't know what it was. But that's the kind of position I would find myself in. Then he said, 'You stay with me, you stay close to me and just ask questions, because you're over this thing.' Whatever it was, whatever my stumbling block was, he understood it, and he came right out in the car and drove right back seventy-five miles."

"The one big thing about Mr. Gurdjieff was that I believed in him. I had absolute trust and faith in him, because in my search I was looking for someone I could trust, and I came upon it. And when I came upon it, I recognized it enough to believe in it. When he told me, 'I'll teach you how to do plumbing,' I believed him."

"He told me, 'You do the plumbing.'"

"'I said, 'I know nothing about it.'"

"He said, 'I'll teach you.' And when he was teaching me he said, 'It's like your body; think of your body: it has supply (the first force), drainage (the second) and ventilation (the third)—those three things. Now you have to go and learn the mechanics.' Isn't that wonderful? That's what I mean when I say I believed in him, so emphatically, no matter what."

"Mme. de Salzmann asked me: 'Frankly, tell me honestly, were you the last one at Prieuré?' 'Yes, I was the last one.' It was closed around 1933 or 1934. I don't know. It was closed when I left, and they went back and forth a couple of times. But I left everything."

"At the end I was the only one there. A fifty-eight-room house. I didn't have a penny. I was in charge of the gate, and then I was in charge of the whole place. It was a fifty-eight-room chateau, on fifty acres! Walled in. I had everything in my possession—all the manuscripts, all the paintings of de Salzmann, all of the music—everything."

"And then I left. I was the last one there. I closed it as much as closing the gate. And then, Mr. Gurdjieff gave me a party. It was a wonderful dinner, like no one had ever experienced. We all drank Armagnac until we were green in the face. And then the Old Man spoke. He made up stories such as, "Prieuré will now close because Benson is leaving," things like that. Of course there was nothing further from the truth than that. I was no force there; I only opened the door. But when I left, he was the only person who came to the train—the Old Man—he didn't want me to leave. I was the only one there he could trust. His no-good family was just no good. He said, 'You can't do this to me.' I said, 'What the hell can I do? I have to leave now, and go home.' I knew his brother and they looked alike, but oh, boy! that man was so vacant of anything—he was like an opaque wall. He was named Dmitri. I had more fights with Dmitri.... He's the man who used to steal all the valuable rugs and sell them. You have no idea what effort it was to bring these rugs from the Near East at that time with the Russian revolution going on. I'd have to go down and buy them back with what little money I had."

"But that wasn't the goal. When I explained the situation to Mr. Gurdjieff, I said, 'It's your brother, he's stealing the rugs out of the study house.' And you know what he used to say to me? 'You shoot him.' Like that. And when I think back, many people alive today would shoot him—'The Old Man said so.'"

"I said, 'No, *you* shoot him, he's your brother. He's your brother, and you shoot him.'"

"'Well, get the rugs back,' he said."

"I said, 'I haven't got any money to get them back.'"

"'Well, you get it,' he said. And I would get it and buy the rugs back … to what end, God only knows, only the effort of putting me on the spot to get the money."

"Because that was my life, not somebody else's. Nobody could ever tell you these stories but me, no matter who the hell they are. They don't know half of the picture. When it comes to any of the group thinking, they're a hierarchy. They don't know anything—not about this, but about anything. They're all Ouspensky people, and this institutionalizing is very Ouspensky. That's the difficulty. It's not for me. So I suggested last year, 'This is not the Gurdjieff Work anymore. We should change the name from the Gurdjieff Foundation to the British Ouspensky People in America Foundation.' Well, Mme. de Salzmann almost died when I said that. The Old Man called the Prieuré 'The Institute,' but it was no more institutional than flying a kite. You lived and starved and somehow you lived."

"The thing that gets under my skin is when people become moralistic. We led an amoral life—a *holy*, amoral life. My life at Prieuré was out of this world."

"I had it out with Mme. de Salzmann last summer. I went down and we sat talking…. She's very much interested in what I'm doing with these tones and sounds and expression. And I said, 'In everything—it doesn't have to be movements, but in the movement of people you're close to and working with and everything—if a whole group can make contact, instead of attempting to do the movements correctly and everybody is out of their existence, there's a definite sound. If a whole group can make contact, there's a definite sound.'"

"She said, 'I know exactly what you mean. We started to do the movements for this film, and then I stopped after a week, and I said we're not getting any place, we're not doing anything, and I think we won't do it anymore.' And then they said, 'Let's have a meeting,' and they sat up all night and talked it all over. The next day, they came in and they were electrified—they hadn't slept. And I heard the sound. There was a definite sound. Then I knew that we could go ahead and make the film.'"

'I said, 'Then you know what I'm attempting.'"

"And she said, 'Oh, absolutely.'"

"But to hear that sound—there's a definite sound there—and until you hear it, you don't know if you're coming or going. It's all mixed up. There won't be any sense until you hear that sound. If you can hear that sound, no matter what happens it'll be right. And that's the way I'm placing my life. I want to hear that sound, and I'm making every effort under the sun. It is not like hearing a bell or anything, but I want to hear that whole place—that ice house—ring as it could. That's what I'm doing down at the ice house in Armonk.

Mme. de Salzmann calls it 'the magicians' workshop,' because we're going to do magic in that place if it kills me. We'll make something odd; we *have* made some odd things. When I was in France this spring, she said, 'Now you talk. Tell them about the ice house.'"

"I said, 'Well, they wouldn't understand that.'"

"'Oh yes,' she said.

"So I said, 'The ice house is the most beautiful building you have ever seen.' And she roared...Mme. de Salzmann just roared. And she said, 'Wait until you see it.'

And I said, 'Well, I think it's beautiful, anyhow.'"

"It's the only place on the whole plantation that could ring, like the Aeolian harp—if there's enough usage and tone coming out of everything, every person and every thing, suddenly you'll hear the sound."

ACKNOWLEDGMENTS

The road leading to the publication of *Martin Benson Speaks* has been long and perilous. The recordings were made more than forty years ago, and, until recently, we assumed they were lost. A handful of people, laboring tirelessly and without hope of reward, have salvaged them from oblivion.

I made the tapes in the last months of Mr. Benson's life. I tried to transcribe them at that time, but the task was beyond me. After his death I stashed them in a box at the back of the hall closet. There they lingered until, some years later, Stanley Isaacs offered to take a shot at transcribing them and I sent him the whole lot. Decades passed. By the time Stanley died I had more or less forgotten about their existence. Then, a few years ago, I learned that Marshall May had gotten Stanley's transcripts and was scanning them. The pages were in a sorry condition, Xerox copies of blurred carbon copies that were sometimes indecipherable. Marshall persevered mightily, and then sent me the pages he'd labored to recover. I showed them to Frank Sinclair who encouraged me to publish them. Later he wrote a foreword to the book.

The tapes had disappeared; no one knew what Stanley had done with them. Requests to Kathy Minnerop, the Foundation archivist, failed to turn anything up. And then, a few months ago, I asked her again. With half closed eyes, as if trying to visualize their place and position, she wondered aloud if she hadn't seen them somewhere recently. She then left the room, and moments later returned and handed me the same cardboard box I'd given to Stanley forty years ago. John Anderson, in a labor of love, was able to copy most of the old, disintegrating tapes onto discs and thus preserve them.

The poet Celestine Frost made a first edit. Roger Lipsey read and commented on it. From several hints he offered, I reordered the text into its present form. Shanti Fader corrected its several iterations. I owe thanks, also, to Alicia Fox for her invaluable advice and help in the execution and production of the design.

Carl Lehmann-Haupt